The Great Opera Companion
Individual Short Guides To
A Hundred Best Operas

GREAT OPERAS
OF PUCCINI

Short Guides to all his Operas

By

Michael Steen

ISBN 978-0-9955385-7-3

Published by Michael Steen, Mattingley, Hampshire, RG27 8JU, 2019, with alterations principally to suit physical form.

Printed and bound in Great Britain by Clays Ltd, Elcograf S.p.A

For

Alma, Helen, William, Eliza, Clementine, Henry,
George, Alexander, Annabel, Harry, Charlie, Toby

CONTENTS

THE GREAT OPERA COMPANION

Great Operas of Puccini – Short Guides to All his Operas is part of an open-ended series entitled *The Great Opera Companion - Individual Short Guides to a Hundred Best Operas*.

This comprises the earlier compendiums: *Great Operas – A Guide to 25 of the World's Finest Musical Experiences; Volume 2, More Great Operas,* which contains another twenty-five; and *Volume 3, Many More Great Operas*, which contains another forty plus several appendices added later. The series also includes *Great Operas of Wagner – Short Guides to All his Operas*.

As the first volume, *Great Operas*, is designed to contain guides to the twenty most popular operas, there is a small amount of duplication between it and the other volumes. The overriding intention is that each chapter in the series is a self-standing guide to an opera. Thus, this results in some duplication of images, and of text, for example the sad story of Doria Manfredi. Although *Great Operas of Puccini* can be read from cover to cover, that is not its primary use

Opera was created and developed to entertain an audience, one way or another, perhaps by being emotional, uplifting, educational, spiritual, or maybe just amusing or delightful. The experience should please, if only because an unpleasing work will not endure. Whether an opera is being experienced in a cinema, an opera-house, or at home on TV, or on radio, the pleasure derived from it is greatly enhanced by understanding and appreciating what it is about, its background, and aspects of the music.

In the Preface to volume 1, the author explained that the guides were originally designed to inform Rosemary, his wife, in a quick, efficient, light and amusing way, about what it helps to know and expect when going to a performance of a particular opera, or when experiencing it electronically in the increasing number of ways available today. People generally find that they do not have time, and there are too many distractions, to inform themselves once they have arrived in the foyer.

A broad-ranging but economical, practical, crisp, and modern guide–a summarisation, a synthesis of a vast amount of available information, selected and presented in a readable form–contributes greatly to appreciation and enjoyment.

Visit www.greatoperas.net to find out more.

THE GREAT OPERA COMPANION:
WHERE IN THE SERIES TO FIND AN OPERA

Key

GO: Great Operas – A Guide to the World's Finest Musical Experiences Volume 1, 'The Top Twenty'

MGO: More Great Operas Volume 2

MMGO: Many More Great Operas Volume 3

GOP: Great Operas of Puccini

GOW: Great Operas of Wagner

Operas marked * are still published as single eGuides.

Beethoven's *Fidelio*, MMGO

Bellini's *Norma*, MGO; *La Sonnambula (The sleepwalker)*, MMGO

Berg's *Wozzeck*, MMGO

Berlioz's *Béatrice et Bénédict*, MGO; *Les Troyens (La Prise de Troie & Les Troyens à Carthage)*, MMGO

Bizet's *Carmen*,* GO; *The Pearl Fishers*, MMGO

Britten's *Peter Grimes*,* GO; *Billy Budd* **MGO**, *Albert Herring* **MMGO**; *A Midsummer Night's Dream*, MGO; *The Rape of Lucretia*, MMGO; *The Turn of the Screw*, MMGO

Cilèa's *Adriana Lecouvreur* MMGO

Debussy's *Pelléas et Mélisande*, MGO

Delibes's *Lakmé*, MMGO

Delius's *A Village Romeo and Juliet*, MMGO

Donizetti's *I Puritani*, MMGO; *L'Elisir d'Amore**, GO; *Lucia di Lammermoor**, GO; *Don Pasquale*, MGO; *La Fille du Régiment*, MGO; *Anna Bolena*, MMGO; *Maria Stuarda*, MMGO

Dvořák's *Rusalka*, MGO

Giordano's *Andrea Chénier*, MMGO

Gluck's *Orfeo ed Euridice*, MGO; *Iphigénie en Aulide*, MMGO; *Iphigénie en Tauride*, MMGO

Gounod's *Faust*, GO; *Roméo et Juliette* MMGO

Handel's *Agrippina*, MMGO; *Rinaldo*, MMGO; *Giulio Cesare*, GO

Humperdinck's *Hänsel und Gretel*, MGO

Janáček's *Jenůfa*, MGO; *Kát'a Kabanová*, MMGO; *The Cunning Little Vixen*, MMGO; *The Makropulos Case*, MMGO

Mascagni's *Cavalleria rusticana*,* & Leoncavallo's *Pagliacci*,* GO

Massenet's *Manon*, MGO; *Don Quichotte*, MMGO; *Werther*, MGO

Monteverdi's *Il Ritorno d'Ulisse in Patria* MMGO; *L'incoronazione di Poppea*, MGO

Mozart's *La Finta Gardiniera*, MMGO; *Die Entführung aus dem Serail (The Abduction from the Seraglio, Il Seraglio)*, MMGO; *Idomeneo*, MMGO; *The Marriage of Figaro*,* GO; *Don Giovanni*,* GO; *Così fan tutte*,* GO; *La Clemenza di Tito*, MMGO; *The Magic Flute*,* GO

Mussorgsky's *Boris Godunov,* MGO
Offenbach's *The Tales of Hoffmann (Les Contes d'Hoffmann),* MMGO
Ponchielli's *La Gioconda* MMGO
Poulenc's *Dialogues des Carmélites,* MGO
Prokofiev's *The Love for Three Oranges,* MMGO
Puccini's *Manon Lescaut; La Bohème;* * *Tosca;* * *Madama Butterfly;* * *La Fanciulla del West; Il Trittico (Il Tabarro, Suor Angelica and Gianni Schicchi); Turandot;* * *Le Villi; Edgar; La Rondine,* ALL IN GOP
Purcell's *Dido and Aeneas* MMGO; *Fairy Queen,* MMGO
Rameau's *Hippolyte et Aricie* MMGO
Ravel's *L'heure espagnole* and *L'enfant et les sortileges,* MMGO
Rossini's *The Barber of Seville,* *GO; *La Cenerentola,* * GO; *L'Italiana in Algeri,* MGO; *Il Turco in Italia* MMGO; *La Donna del Lago,* MMGO; *Le Comte Ory & Il Viaggio a Reims,* MMGO; *Guillaume Tell (William Tell),* MMGO
Saint-Saëns's *Samson et Dalila,* MMGO
Shostakovich's *Lady Macbeth of Mtsensk* MMGO
Smetana's *The Bartered Bride,* MGO
Johann Strauss's *Die Fledermaus,* GO
Richard Strauss's *Der Rosenkavalier,* MMGO; *Salome,* MGO; *Elektra,* MGO; *Ariadne auf Naxos,* MGO; *Die Frau ohne Schatten,* MMGO; *Intermezzo,* MMGO; *Arabella,* MMGO; *Capriccio,* MMGO
Stravinsky's *The Rake's Progress,* MMGO
Tchaikovsky's *Eugene Onegin,* * GO; *The Queen of Spades,* MMGO
Verdi's *Nabucco,* MMGO; *I Due Foscari,* MMGO; *Macbeth,* MMGO; *Rigoletto,* * GO; *Il Trovatore,* * GO; *La Traviata,* * GO; *Aïda,* * GO; *Simon Boccanegra,* MMGO; *Un Ballo in Maschera,* MGO; *Don Carlo,* MGO; *The Sicilian Vespers,* MGO; *La Forza del Destino,* MMGO; *Otello,* MMGO; *Falstaff,* MMGO
Wagner's Early Operas *(Die Feen, Das Liebesverbot, Rienzi); Tannhäuser,* * GO; *The Flying Dutchman; Lohengrin; Tristan und Isolde,* * GO; *Die Meistersinger (The Mastersingers);The Ring of the Nibelung: Das Rheingold, Die Walküre, Siegfried* and *Götterdämmerung; Parsifal,* ALL IN GOW
Weber's *Der Freischütz,* MGO

USING THIS BOOK

A quick grasp of each opera and its context can be gained by reading the opening section on BACKGROUND and the following WHO'S WHO and WHAT'S WHAT. The section on TALKING POINTS is intended to increase the reader's general appreciation of the work. In particular, the opera-goer who has read it will be more knowledgeable when socialising and thus will enjoy the opera experience more.

Particularly for those who want to dig deeper, further elaboration, including easily digestible information about various aspects of the music, may be found in ACT by ACT.

The patience of an audience and a reader can wear thin; a Short Guide should be short. As the nineteenth and twentieth century progressed, various libretti became more complicated and lengthy. In some cases, WHO'S WHO and WHAT'S WHAT may generally be found to provide sufficient information for the opera-goer.

Today, countless musical examples are easily and instantly available through Google. Historical recordings of individual specific items can be heard by searching a few words of an aria or other item, and following the link.

ABOUT THE AUTHOR

Michael Steen OBE was born in Dublin. He studied at the Royal College of Music, and was the organ scholar at Oriel College, Oxford. Opera has been one of his great pleasures. During a successful thirty year career in the City of London, and afterwards, he has met many who go to it, thus gaining considerable insight into the information which it helps to know in order to enhance one's appreciation and enjoyment of the opera experience. He has been the chairman of the RCM Society and of the Friends of the V&A Museum, the Treasurer of The Open University, and a trustee of Anvil Arts, The Gerald Coke Handel Foundation and of The Royal College of Organists.

BY THE AUTHOR

The Lives and Times of the Great Composers (eBook and hardcopy)
Great Operas – A Guide to 25 of the World's Finest Musical Experiences – Volume 1 (eBook and hardcopy)
Great Operas of Puccini – Short Guides to all his Operas (eBook and hardcopy)
Great Operas of Wagner – Short Guides to all his Operas (eBook and hardcopy)
More Great Operas – A Guide to 25 more of the World's Finest Musical Experiences – Volume 2 (eBook)
Many More Great Operas – A Guide to 40 More of the World's Finest Musical Experiences – Volume 3 including Appendices (eBook)
Enchantress of Nations: Pauline Viardot, Soprano, Muse and Lover (hardcopy)

Puccini in Vienna with Jeritza,
the greatly admired Tosca, Minnie and Turandot

Manon Lescaut

The young Puccini

CONTENTS

MANON LESCAUT: BACKGROUND

Manon Lescaut placed Puccini firmly 'on the operatic map and was the foundation of his international fame', although it was not his first opera.[1]

He had already passed the age of thirty and was in need of a success when his *Edgar* flopped. Nevertheless, that opera showed sufficient promise for his backer Giulio Ricordi, the influential Milanese publisher who was to be 'the architect of his career', to continue to support him financially despite pressure from his firm's shareholders to drop him.

In a daring move, Puccini felt that he could succeed with a 'Manon'.

The story had been used several times already, by leading composers.[2] A few years earlier, the French composer Jules Massenet had had a 'phenomenal success' with it. Eighteen years before that, there had been a *Manon Lescaut* by Auber, the composer of the outstandingly successful grand opera *La Muette de Portici*. There was a ballet as well; and similar ground had been covered in the 1830s with Michael Balfe's *The Maid of Artois*, which starred the great soprano Maria Malibran.

Most importantly, the financial pedigree was excellent: Massenet's opera had enabled him to become 'one of the richest musicians of his time'. Puccini hoped that his version would ensure him the 'handsome income' for which he craved and which he thought he deserved. It did.

The well-known classic novel, *Les Aventures du Chevalier des Grieux et de Manon Lescaut*,[3] had been written in the eighteenth century by the French author Abbé Prévost. The fictional Des Grieux was a seventeen year-old student when the stage coach arrived in Amiens taking Manon away to become a nun. In the novel, he has returned home after her death, and he tells the story to someone who, two years earlier, had kindly lent him some money when he followed Manon and the other prostitutes on their way to transportation from Le Havre to America.

'Officially', the novel may have provided a 'cautionary tale' about the conflict between reason and passion, virtue and vice; about the struggle of a man between instinct and his better self.

---

1 His first opera was *Le Villi*.

2 The tale endures: in 1952, Hans-Werner Henze's opera *Boulevard Solitude*, based on the same story, was premièred.

3 The 'n' at the end of 'Manon' may be sounded in Italian but not in French. The 't' in Lescaut is silent, so the name sounds like 'Lessko'. Des Grieux is pronounced approximately like 'Day Gree-ēr'.

But it was also a rollicking good story of elopement, sex, gambling, violence, murder, escape, and death. The novel was banned by the authorities when it was published. Even half a century ago, it was not considered suitable reading for secondary-school children in England. It was irrelevant that the 'deux enfants' intended to get married when they ran off to Paris: she was a courtesan[4] – worse, just a common prostitute! – and the description of her world, her beautiful body, her lack of constancy and her overpowering love of wealth, was immoral.

For Puccini, the preparation of his libretto based on this story became a nightmare. Ricordi first asked Leoncavallo, who would shortly gain international fame for his one-act opera *Pagliacci*, to write the libretto for him. But Puccini did not like the result. So several playwrights, journalists, and the like, were subsequently involved over a protracted period of time.

After a draft was available in summer of 1890, Puccini, who loved the countryside, went to a small village on the Swiss border, near Chiasso,[5] in order to compose. But it would take him three years to finish the work. Probably rightly, he was obsessed with the need for his opera to be different from Massenet's – even to the extent of wanting a wholly different title. But Ricordi pointed out that it would be absurd for such a well-known story to be called anything other than 'Manon'. They compromised with 'Manon Lescaut', a title which Puccini chose in order to distinguish his opera from Massenet's.

He continued to have trouble with the libretto. He was a painstaking perfectionist with a 'sensational flair for theatrical effect'. He knew what he wanted and he was utterly determined to have his own way. In the end, so many pens were involved that it was decided not to acknowledge any individual librettist and the opera is simply entitled 'Giacomo Puccini, Manon Lescaut, Dramma lirico in quattro atti'. The journalist and playwright George Bernard Shaw summed it up: 'he has arranged his own libretto from Prévost'.

---

4 Mistresses were of course a normal feature of life, Louis XV leading the way with his. Courtesans, *les grandes horizontales*, were a particular feature of Paris a century later, and have tended to be glamorised, as in Verdi's *La Traviata*. A courtesan is less than a mistress because she sells her love for material benefits; but she is more than a prostitute because the demand for her services is such that she can choose her lovers.

5 Ruggiero Leoncavallo (1857–1919) had taken the chalet opposite. He displayed a canvas depicting a clown (Pagliacci) on his door; so Puccini displayed a white hand (Manon, in Italian) on his. Leoncavallo was born in Naples, the son of a police magistrate. He was fond of his food, overweight and good-natured. Only *Pagliacci*, which remains one of the most widely performed operas worldwide, has survived of his twenty operas and operettas.

The opera was composed partly in the chalet near Chiasso, partly in Lucca and partly in Torre del Lago, the village near Lucca where Puccini would eventually make his home.

Puccini finished it in October 1892, after leaving act 3, the 'Embarkation scene' to be completed last. His score, with its large numbers of crossings out, pastings over and other changes, testifies to the immense trouble he took. Indeed, there is some difficulty in determining what he finally wanted: there are six different editions of the Italian vocal score.

Manon Lescaut was premièred at the Teatro Regio, in Turin, on 1 February, 1893, nine months after Leoncavallo's success with his *Pagliacci*.

Turin was chosen rather than Milan because the Milanese audience might be prejudiced against Puccini after the earlier failure of his *Edgar* there. But the decision was no doubt greatly influenced by the imminent première, in Milan, of Verdi's *Falstaff*, which would take place eight days later.

Puccini's understandable apprehension was unnecessary. His première was a tremendous success: he would never have another first night like it. The critics liked the fact that the opera was neither trivially melodramatic, nor excessively serious like Wagner's operas. It was something they could recognise as truly Italian. At a banquet held in his honour, all he could splutter was 'Grazie a tutti!'

London saw *Manon Lescaut* fifteen months later. Three months after that, there was a performance in English in Philadelphia. However it only reached New York in 1898 when it was performed in Wallack's Theater.

The London reception was comparatively cool, possibly because the title role was performed by a soprano who was 'just a little too ladylike', and the 'conventional operatic death scene was so unconvincing'. It is also considerably less lyrical than Massenet's version. Despite this, the production led George Bernard Shaw to write: 'Puccini looks to me more like the heir of Verdi than any of his rivals'. And he was correct.

The stunningly beautiful Lina Cavalieri was the first Manon Lescaut at the Met.
She was killed in Italy in 1944 in an Allied bombing raid.

Commentators are, however, inclined to rate *Manon Lescaut* behind Massenet's version: 'Massenet's Manon is a masterpiece, which Puccini's is not', so it is said. But *Manon* is mature Massenet whereas *Manon Lescaut* is youthful Puccini. It is perhaps curious that, in Puccini's version, there is no blockbuster. There is no 'big and memorable tune', which became such a feature of his later works.

The part of Manon Lescaut has been performed by many divas, including Callas. It has however given some distinguished sopranos some difficulty. Of the two whores, Carmen attracts all the sympathy, whereas Manon gets little. The 'seductive but perfidious woman', 'cette charmante et perfide créature' is so mercenary, that it is difficult to warm to her. Some commentators argue that it is idiotic to criticise her – hers is a wholly realistic portrait, but in the opera she is somewhat two dimensional, at least when compared to Massenet's Manon.

Manon's Cavaliere des Grieux carries conviction in the book, in which the story is 'told' by him and essentially about him. A seventeen year-old student might be expected to erupt with 'un example terrible de la force de ses passions'. But no youth of that age could possibly sing this immensely difficult role, a veritable tour-de-force which has necessarily become the preserve of tenors of riper years, such as Björling, Caruso, Domingo and Pavarotti. Unfortunately, the tenors at times justify the

6

comment that 'what was ardent passion on Verdi's stage is more like hysteria on Puccini's'.

Puccini's characterisation is full-blooded. He does not hold back on his instructions: there are countless expression markings.[6] Still, the hectic fast-moving passages and the 'enervating languor in the slow music', reflect the character of the composer, and provide enjoyable entertainment.

At the Met, the first Renato des Grieux was Caruso

---

6 Markings abound such as 'dolcissimo', 'estremamente piano', 'con grande passione', 'con disperazione', 'con ultimo sforzo', 'colla massima angoscia', 'con immense angoscia', 'con calore', 'con tutta la passione'. Just before Manon dies, although weak and breathless, 'af-fannando, con voce debolissima', she smiles and sings 'con ineffabile dolcezza'.

Who's Who and What's What

This summary is based on the libretto. As mentioned in the Warning at the end of this book, certain directors may amend opera stories to suit their production.

Outside the inn in Amiens,[7] **Edmondo**, a student and would-be poet, is prominent among his boisterous friends enjoying their drink. A more thoughtful and sober student, Cavaliere **Renato des Grieux**, joins them shortly before the stagecoach comes in from Arras. Out of it steps **Lescaut** (a sergeant of the Royal guard), with his stunningly beautiful sister **Manon Lescaut** who is destined for a convent.[8] With them is the rich and elderly tax farmer,[9] **Geronte di Ravoir** (the Treasurer-General).

Manon (who introduces herself with *Manon Lescaut mi chiamo*) and des Grieux instantly fall in love with each other. He is ecstatic: *Dio, quanto è bella!...Donna non vidi mai.* Geronte has arranged with the **innkeeper** for a carriage in which he can abscond with Manon, but des Grieux beats him to it and the young couple elopes to Paris.

Sometime later, Manon has deserted des Grieux for the wealth and luxury which Geronte can provide in Paris for both her as a courtesan and her brother as her pimp. A **Perruquier** (a mime) attends to her hair; **Musicians** perform before her, and a **Ballet master** gives her lessons. But when des Grieux appears, Manon's passion for him is rekindled. They are caught 'in flagrante' by Geronte who summons the **Sergeant** of the archers to arrest Manon.

In act 3, Manon awaits transportation to Louisiana. She is on the quayside in Le Havre, together with other convicted prostitutes. A **Lamplighter** provides some contrast. An attempted escape arranged by Lescaut fails. In desperation, des Grieux persuades the **Marine Captain** to let him accompany him as a servant on board ship to America.

In Louisiana, things do not work out for the lovers. They find themselves in the desert near New Orleans. They are short of water and, after she sings her popular aria *Sola, perduta, abbandonnata,* Manon dies.

---

7 Amiens is about ninety miles north-west of Paris. Arras is about forty miles south east of Amiens. Le Havre is a port on the Channel coast, one hundred and twenty-five miles from Paris, due south of London.

8 A description of her as a 'convent-bound waif' seems wide of the mark. In Massenet's opera, she is later said to be just sixteen.

9 The 'ferme' was a means of collecting taxes. In 1726, a contract was made with forty 'fermiers généraux' who guaranteed the King eighty million livres a year. From what they raised, they kept the very considerable surplus. Many tax farmers ended their lives on the scaffold in the French Revolution.

TALKING POINTS

Giacomo Puccini (1858–1924)
Please see the summary of the life of Puccini on pages 159 and 160.

Puccini's Place as a Composer – a View
The view expressed on pages 161-163 is very relevant.

Abbé Prévost
Antoine François Prévost d'Exilles (1697–1763) was 'one of the most important French novelists of the eighteenth century'. Although one modern commentator has said that he 'was little more than a prolific hack', *Les Aventures du Chevalier des Grieux et de Manon Lescaut* has been called 'his masterpiece'. 'I had almost as soon omit *The Vicar of Wakefield* or *The Pilgrim's Progress* from my bookshelf as *Manon Lescaut*', wrote George Bernard Shaw.

Prévost was born about thirty-five miles from Arras in Northern France. He came from a legal family, was educated by Jesuits, and then fluctuated between being a soldier and a monk. At the age of thirty, he decamped from a scholarly Benedictine community and went to London where he became an anglophile. Later, he moved to Amsterdam. Possibly he had converted to Protestantism. Also at this time, he may have 'contracted a regular, or rather irregular, marriage'.

'Manon Lescaut' (1731) was volume VII appended to his 'Mémoires d'un Homme de Qualité' (1728).

His Manon has been described as 'one of the most remarkable heroines in all fiction. She has no literary ancestress; she seems to have sprung entirely from his imagination, or perhaps his sympathetic observation'. Possibly the theme echoed things in Prévost's own life which he had felt very deeply: her character may have been based on that of his Hungarian mistress, Lenki Eckhardt.

Prévost also wrote a periodical, *Le Pour et le Contre*, part literary review, part in the style of Addison's *Spectator*. He returned to France, was allowed to wear the dress of a secular priest and was attached to the royal household of the Prince de Conti. His output, which included translations of Richardson's *Pamela* and *Clarissa*, was vast, comprising almost forty volumes.

He was said to have been struck with apoplexy when out on a walk near the small cottage in which he lived at Chantilly, just to the north of Paris. The local surgeon unfortunately conducted a premature post-mortem, as a consequence of which Prévost died.

Between Puccini's acts and scenes

The events between the elopement at the end of Puccini's act 1 and des Grieux's entry into Manon's residence in act 2 take up well over two-thirds of Prévost's text. Librettists and composers usually have to compress the story on which an opera is based, and literary value can be lost in the process. In Puccini's opera, much is indeed lost.

The part of the story which Puccini ignores is the titillating kind of material that sells well today. Prévost wrote in the enjoyably racy, lewd and witty style also found in English literature of the time, whether in Fielding's *Tom Jones*, Richardson's *Pamela*, or even Cleland's *Fanny Hill*. However, it is French and subtle, rather than pornographic.

The initial love-affair between Manon and des Grieux does not last long. His character crumbles as, driven by relentless passion, he remains constant to his wholly unfaithful, dissolute mistress whose focus is on wealth and pleasure.[10]

The girl destined for a convent is faithful for around twelve days. Within three weeks she is seduced by a rich neighbour. Des Grieux is fetched home by his brother and given a dressing-down by his father. After cooling off, he goes to Paris to study to become a priest.

---

10 In her favour, it was said that 'elle pèche sans malice', she sins without malice.

Two years after the elopement from Amiens, Manon, by then a courtesan in Paris, still only in her eighteenth year, hears that des Grieux is presenting a religious dissertation. Out of curiosity, she goes along to listen. They resume their affair and set up together with the loot which she has filched from lovers.

She runs through the fortune; Lescaut, her unpleasant brother, comes and sponges off them. Then their house goes on fire and, in the mêlée, the remains of their money is stolen.

To maintain Manon's life-style, des Grieux takes up gambling, and cheating. But one day he returns to find a letter from her saying she has gone off with another wealthy admirer. However, des Grieux pretends to be Manon's young brother, a trainee cleric who is lodging with her. The two of them abscond when the wealthy lover goes to prepare himself for the night's activities. But they are arrested. Manon is taken to the Salpêtrière prison for prostitutes.

After three months inside the St Lazare prison, des Grieux escapes, killing the gatekeeper as he goes. He then gets Manon out of her prison, dressed as a man.

It is not long before des Grieux learns that, while he is away gambling, Manon is going out with an Italian prince. Subsequently, Manon and des Grieux hatch a new plan to elope. But she fails to turn up for the rendezvous, and sends him another whore as her substitute.

Nothing much changes. Des Grieux and Manon arrange to have her next lover kidnapped, so that des Grieux can enjoy the night in his bed. But when the kidnap takes place, the lover's father is informed. He storms in to the bedroom just as the guilty couple are about to begin their tryst. As des Grieux candidly observes, a man in his underwear is defenceless. The father first seizes the opportunity to make a pass at Manon; then he has them taken off again to prison.

Des Grieux manages to enlist his own father's help to persuade the other old man to bribe the police-chief to order his release. But there is a condition: Manon is either to stay in prison for life, or to be transported immediately to America.

As in the opera, des Grieux has no difficulty getting on the ship because the authorities want young men to go and populate the colonies. Unfortunately, on arrival, the nephew of the Governor falls for Manon, which is fair enough as she is still unmarried. Des Grieux fights him in a duel and thinks he has killed him, hence their hurried escape in the direction of the English colonies. (This explains the tragedy which unfolds in Puccini's act 4.) It turns out that the nephew has only been wounded, and des Grieux is able to makes his way back to France after Manon's death.

The libretto – more about the chaos

The preparation of the libretto was chaotic. After Puccini rejected Leoncavallo's libretto, he instructed the popular playwright Marco Praga to write it. So as to avoid this being too like the *Manon* of Massenet, he required him to follow the novel rather than the French libretto. Praga brought in the journalist and politician Domenico Oliva to help with the versification.

Although Puccini had liked their draft, it soon drove him to despair. When he wanted to cut out material about the two lovers eking a living in penury in Paris, Praga withdrew, leaving Oliva to carry on. He and Puccini produced the Embarkation act, the first of Puccini's big tableaux in his operas.

But Puccini fell out with Oliva who also pulled out. Ricordi turned to the distinguished playwright Giuseppe Giacosa, who had previously provided Puccini with a libretto which had been rejected. Giacosa was unenthusiastic, so, to complete the libretto of *Manon Lescaut*, he introduced Luigi Illica, a rough republican. This improbable and quarrelsome team would later create *La Bohème*, *Tosca* and *Madama Butterfly*. Illica introduced the roles of the Hairdresser, the Music Master, the Dancing Master and the Lamplighter. But Puccini quarrelled with Illica, and Giacosa had to intervene. Ricordi, ever the diplomat, also calmed them down.

Giulio Ricordi and the 'holy trinity'

Giulio Ricordi (1840–1912), the leading publisher and a minor composer, held immense power as 'king-maker and eminence grise' in the musical world. His firm had been founded and developed in Milan in 1808 by his grandfather Giovanni; and it was further developed under his father Tito. Its initial success and strength arose from it being the official publisher of the music performed at La Scala. By publishing Verdi's *Oberto* around fifteen years earlier, the firm took 'the most significant single step in the entire history of the firm'. By the time of Giovanni's death in 1853, it had had issued twenty-five thousand publications.

For Giulio, so adept and ruthless at managing the firm's relationship with his artists, Verdi was 'god'. His works and those of Puccini have been Ricordi's most valuable asset. To maintain the relationship after a fiasco with Puccini's second opera, *Edgar*, Giulio even personally guaranteed Puccini's debt to the firm. He was not always right: he failed to spot Bizet,

---

Mascagni and Leoncavallo. Conversely, Sonzogno, the firm's 'strongest' rival, turned down Puccini's *Le Villi*.

The firm was sometimes criticised for being too commercial and for issuing poor quality publications. (Amazingly, it has been claimed that there were 27,000 errors in Verdi's *Falstaff*.) The retirement in 1919 of Giulio's son **Tito Ricordi** (1865–1933) 'the younger', brought to an end the family's management of the firm. The oldest of Giulio's four children, he had joined his father. He fell out with Puccini over *La Rondine*. Unlike his father, with whom he quarrelled frequently, he was arrogant, 'impulsive, short-tempered, and dictatorial'. He was very energetic and was one of the first to appreciate the importance of good acting and careful production.

* * *

Giulio Ricordi called Puccini and his librettists, Illica and Giacosa, the 'holy trinity'.

At a young age, **Luigi Illica** (1857–1919) fought at sea against the Turks. Later, in Milan, he moved in literary and radical circles. His first play was written in conjunction with Fontana, the librettist of Puccini's *Le Villi* and *Edgar*. (Fontana was another republican, and eventually ended his life in exile.) Illica wrote thirty-five libretti. He drank heavily and was irascible.

Giuseppe Giacosa (1847–1906), the son of a lawyer, gave up the legal profession. He became professor of literature and dramatic art at the Milan Conservatoire, and by the end of his life was respected as Italy's leading playwright. Benign and calm, he was very conscientious and painstaking. In summary, Illica provided the scenario and sense of theatre; Giacosa provided the poetry, shape and balance. Puccini called him 'my best of poets, mender of other men's faults'. His poetic artistry and insight into the female psyche enabled him to highlight and enhance the lyrical moments.

At the violently stormy meetings in Ricordi's office, where they discussed the various projects, Giacosa contributed a soothing influence, and he became known as the Buddha. But Giacosa himself experienced moments of intense frustration.

After Giacosa's death, Illica did not produce another successful libretto for Puccini: they fell out over the project for an opera about Queen Marie Antoinette which never came to fruition.

Massenet's *Manon*

Manon is the best-known of Massenet's operas. With it, he became France's most popular composer. It was first performed at the Opéra-Comique in Paris in 1884. Today, it is also performed as a ballet, with choreography by Kenneth MacMillan.

Jules Massenet (1842–1912) mass-produced twenty further operas after *Manon* – 'always on the look-out for ways to add a bit of spice to what remained fundamentally the same musical recipe'. His operas include *Werther*, *Thaïs* (with the well-known *Méditation*), and a Cinderella. They are generally of a single brand, 'a sort of amorous epic poem' with 'much sentimentalism, an atmosphere of sighs, caresses, spasms and tears'. The moment in history is always different, but the music is similar. He himself said: 'The public likes it and we must always agree with the public'.

Sibyl Sanderson: Massenet's Manon

The story in act 1 of Massenet's *Manon*, outside the inn in Amiens, is very similar to Puccini's.[11] It contains her 'chic little song' addressed to her cousin Lescaut, *Je suis encore étourdie*, and a tuneful duet with des Grieux, in which she tells of her love of pleasure and her family's determination to send her to a convent. He persuades her, reluctantly, to leave for Paris with him.

---

11 Puccini's opera is entirely through-composed, whereas at times Massenet's characters speak while the orchestra continues.

Subsequent acts are different and more detailed, although the outcome, her death, is the same. In Massenet's act 2, in the cosy love-nest, des Grieux writes to his father to ask permission to marry Manon. They are visited by her brother and a nobleman who wants her. With her connivance, they seize des Grieux. But not before she has sung the 'best tune', *Adieu notre petite table*, anticipating her departure. This is followed by des Grieux describing his dream about the cosy cottage in which they will live, *Le Rève de Manon*.

Time moves on. The Paris market is *en fête*, Manon, a rich courtesan, overhears des Grieux's father describing how his son has entered a seminary. She inquires for news of her lover. During the ballet, a standard feature in French opera, she realises that she must see him.

Des Grieux resists his father's attempt to persuade him to find a 'nice' girl to marry, rather than take holy orders: *Ah fuyez douce image*, Begone lovely dream. Manon arrives at his seminary as the Magnificat is being sung. The audience is provided with Massenet's potent mixture, sex and religion, as she falls to her knees, a repentant Magdalen. Des Grieux resists, but she implores: *N'est-ce plus ma main que cette main presse*.

Massenet's act 4 is set in a gambling house, populated by a chorus of card-sharps. When des Grieux wins consistently, he is accused of cheating. The lovers are arrested: *O douleur, l'avenir nous sépare*. In walks his father, who says that des Grieux should be arrested and she be taken to the prostitutes' prison.

In Massenet's act 5, des Grieux hopes to attack the convoy of prisoners on their way to Le Havre, but the guards are too well armed. The sergeant is bribed to let Manon out overnight. She is too exhausted to flee and she dies in her lover's arms, in France.

It needs a Frenchman to conjure up the French atmosphere. Almost every French composer either followed Massenet's style or loathed it. One condemned it as 'discreet and pseudo-religious eroticism'. Massenet had a great influence on Puccini.

ACT BY ACT

Act 1 Amiens in the eighteenth century: outside an inn
The hustle and bustle near the gate leading to Paris is depicted in the orchestral introduction, which includes various themes which recur in the act.

Edmondo and his fellow students fool around, drink, watch the world go by and flirt with the girls. His friend, a more reserved student, Renato des Grieux turns up. He is moody, and uninterested in Love: *L'amor! Questa tragedia.* But he pretends to flirt, to the amusement of the students: *Tra voi, belle, brune e bionde.*

The sound of the post-horn signals the arrival of the stage-coach from Arras. The passengers step out. They include Lescaut, who is a sergeant of the King's guard, together with his sister Manon, and Geronte de Ravoir, the Treasurer-General. The students ogle the beautiful Manon. The innkeeper sorts out the luggage.

For des Grieux, it is love at first sight: *Dio, quanto è bella!* The duet includes her reply (so simple, yet requiring such careful phrasing) *Manon Lescaut mi chiamo*, My name is Manon Lescaut. He is aghast when she tells him that she is on the way to a convent, as arranged by her father, and she is due to leave at dawn. She is called away by her brother, but promises to return when darkness falls.

Des Grieux has never seen such a beautiful girl: *Donna non vidi mai* has been described as 'one of the most ecstatic of Puccini's great tenor arias'. For him, the words *Manon Lescaut mi chiamo* are like perfume. Edmondo and the students are highly amused by all this and continue to flirt with the girls.

Geronte and Lescaut discuss Manon. Lescaut indicates that he agrees with his father's decision to send her to a convent. Geronte (who is characterised by low lying discords) invites him to dine. Geronte must first make some 'arrangements' with the innkeeper.

Lescaut joins the students playing cards, and gets increasingly inebriated. Edmondo overhears Geronte ordering the innkeeper to have a coach ready in an hour, and observes him going to inspect the exit behind the tavern. The host rubs his hands with glee at the thought of the money. Edmondo warns des Grieux that his flower is about to be plucked from under his nose by the old man.

Manon reappears and tells des Grieux that she has returned to him although her conscience bade her otherwise: *Vedete? Io son fedele.* She

16

is sad, leaving her happy home, but the happy times are now all over. He says he loves her and will save her from Geronte who is about to abduct her. Edmondo, who is greatly amused by the prank, tells them that the coach is ready. They climb in and head off to Paris.

Geronte returns. He tells the innkeeper that it is time to leave and pretends to order supper. He is horrified to hear from Edmondo that the girl has already gone: he has been beaten to it by a student!

In a chorus with the soloists soaring above, the students have a laugh at Geronte's expense and to his annoyance. Lescaut confides to him that he need not worry, because no student will be able to finance his sister's expensive tastes in Paris: *Parigi! È là Manon*. Geronte can have Manon if he makes the right offer. He encourages him to relax and enjoy his supper.

Act 2 Geronte's palatial residence in Paris

The very restrained first half of this act[12] enables 'the emotional temperature to rise in a steep curve' in the second half. The act opens with Manon having her hair done by the Perruquier, who she bosses around. She and her brother Lescaut are onto a good thing: she is a courtesan in great luxury; he is living off her 'earnings'. He admires her at her toilette, and advises her which beauty spots to affix. She is his creation, and he claims credit for having saved her from a penniless student, who would have sustained her with nothing more than kisses: *Sei splendida*. Des Grieux may be a nice boy, but he is not the Treasurer-General.

Manon however longs for des Grieux, who she abandoned without so much as a kiss: *In quelle trine morbide*. Surrounded by riches and silks, she feels incarcerated in a chilly tomb.[13]

Lescaut knows that des Grieux also longs for her, and imitates him. Lescaut has told him that he would have had a better chance if he had possessed more money, and has advised him to take up gambling. She continues to pine for des Grieux, but she is distracted by seeing her beautiful reflection in the mirror.

To entertain her, musicians, led by a mezzo-soprano, perform a 'madrigal' *Sulla vetta tu del monte*, which has been composed by Geronte as a homage to her. (Puccini sourced this from the *Agnus Dei* of a Mass

12 The change in scene constitutes 'an unbelievable jump'. 'The little ingénue we met at Amiens' is now a flashy courtesan, already tired of her protector, the old roué, the Treasurer-General. When Puccini dropped an act which he originally envisaged set in a cosy love-nest in Paris, the continuity was broken, improbably. *Parigi! È là Manon* was inserted at the end of act 1, at the instigation of Illica, after the première, in order to paper over this gap.

13 She reaches top B flat and eventually a sustained top C. She also reaches C in *L'ora O Tirsi*.

which he had composed as a student.) In the 'madrigal', Geronte praises her beauty and longs for her to be his. Lescaut keeps the tip which she intends for the musicians.

Geronte has invited his old cronies to join him and to salivate at his conquest. A dancing master, Il maestro di ballo, teaches Manon a minuet. During this, Lescaut ponders the risk inherent in her boredom, and he goes to see if he can make use of des Grieux in some way so as to alleviate it.

Manon is annoyed by the ogling of the lascivious cronies. The dancing master calls for a cavalier. Geronte, who is bowled over by her, obliges. She compliments Geronte, *L'ora O Tirsi*.

He then invites them all in to supper. The guests leave with bowings and scrapings, giving Puccini the opportunity for another fine chorus with soloists.

* * *

Manon admires herself in the mirror, *O, sarò la più bella!* She sees a man entering, who she first thinks is a lackey. But it is des Grieux. There is a sudden change in tempo and mood.

But she is taken aback by his coldness towards her. He reproaches her for causing him so much suffering: *Taci, taci, tu il cor mio frangi*. She pleads with him. She demonstrates her materialism by promising to share her new-found wealth with him, and by admiring her own beauty. She lures him: Come my love, enfold in your arms Manon who loves you, *Vieni! Colle tue braccia stringi Manon che t'ama*. He is bewitched by this temptress, *O tentatrice*. They sink onto the sofa.[14]

They are interrupted by an astonished Geronte: *Affè, madamigella*. She intervenes when des Grieux tries to go for him. Manon mocks Geronte by holding up a mirror to him and comparing him with des Grieux. Geronte says he knows when it is time to leave: but he will be back! *Addio, bell'idol mio*.

They know that they must escape, though she does not want to leave her assets behind. Des Grieux is sliding down the slippery slope to perdition, card-sharping and crime. *Ah Manon, mi tradisce*: Dirt in the dirt am I.

---

14 This section has been said to contain some of the most passionate pages Puccini ever penned. It has considerable Wagnerian overtones, as, in their transports, the lovers refer to dying and yearning, language redolent of *Tristan and Isolde*. In this passage, as in the Intermezzo which follows, Puccini quotes the 'Tristan' chord, a very distinctive discordant chord, used by Wagner in the Prelude and the love-music of his opera.

18

Will she really want to share this life with him? But instead of escaping, the lovers fall into each others arms again.

With tremendous urgency, for which Puccini uses a fugue, Lescaut tells them to go: Geronte has called the guards, and Manon will be transported into exile if she is apprehended. But she continues to delay, and empties drawers and collects up her jewelry and other items which she is reluctant to leave. They are about to escape into the garden. But it is too late. The soldiers arrive and arrest her. Geronte lets out a laugh. All the jewels fall onto the floor.

There is an orchestral intermezzo, *La prigionia – Il viaggio all'Havre*, Captivity, the road to Le Havre. During this, we can reflect on the fate of a fool and a tart. This fills in another big gap in the action.

Act 3 The harbour at Le Havre[15]

Lescaut and des Grieux are outside the barracks where Manon is being held before boarding a Man o' War for transportation to Louisiana. Des Grieux is distraught and nervous, pursued as he is by dark fate. But Lescaut is confident, because he has bribed the guard: at dawn, Manon will be free. The guard is changed.

Des Grieux assures Manon, who is behind bars, that he has not forsaken her: *Tu amore? Amore? Ah Manon disperato*: Soon she will be his. They are interrupted by a lamplighter singing a little song.

The call 'To Arms' informs us that unfortunately Lescaut's escape plan has failed. Lescaut tells des Grieux to run away. Even Manon implores him to do so.

The girls in chains are brought along, and the Captain of the Man o' War tells the Sergeant to do the roll-call. As the girls are called, some are insolent, some crest-fallen, others are indignant. The crowd, especially the women, comment, sometimes spitefully. When Lescaut tells the crowd that des Grieux is Manon's husband, and she was abducted, the people answer, to his annoyance, 'They all say that'. But in a fond farewell, rising to top C, Manon tells her lover that they must part for ever and he must give up the thought of her. The tolling of the big drum adds to the colour. This chorus with soloists is worthy of Verdi.

The sergeant marshals the girls, *Presto, in fila*. He seizes Manon, and pushes des Grieux away. At first, des Grieux tries to stop Manon being

---

15 George Bernard Shaw was complimentary about the Embarkation scene. Referring to two leading librettists, he wrote that Puccini 'has served himself as well as Scribe ever served Meyerbeer, or Boito Verdi'.

taken. Then, he capitulates and in *Guardate, pazzo son, guardate*, he implores the Captain to take him as his servant. The Captain agrees, because America needs populating. Des Grieux and Manon are delighted. And the love theme from act 2 is thundered out.

Act 4 The desert in Louisiana

It is night-time on the border of the territory of New Orleans. Des Grieux[16] tries to support the exhausted Manon. She recovers. He weeps; he finds she has a fever, *Vedi, vedi, son io che piango*. She gazes at him as if she does not recognise him; and she is overcome with thirst, *Sei tu che piangi?* But all he sees is arid wasteland.[17]

She tells him that she will rest for a bit, and that he should go ahead and find shelter. We hear the love theme again. Puccini now gives her a great aria to sing. Distraught and lonely, she is beyond hope, *Sola, perduta, abbandonnata*. She sought this region as a haven; her beauty has been her disaster. She does not want to die. But it is too late. She becomes increasingly delirious, and desperate.

Her lover returns, having found nothing but dry, relentless desert. He tries to make her rest. She can hardly speak, except to say that she loves him. He is horrified that she is dying. He observes that the chill of death *Gelo di morte!* is on her. We hark quickly back to the minuet of the dancing lesson. He weeps and cannot bear to be left behind to live without her. They kiss. She says that Time will extinguish her faults, but her love will never die. She dies in his arms. Convulsed with grief, he sobs uncontrollably.[18]

---

16 Enrico Caruso when first performing this work was only given three days notice, far too little time to memorise this demanding role. He performed the death scene with his vocal score propped up against Manon's bottom. Both singers rise to top C in this act.

17 New Orleans was flooded by the Mississippi following hurricane Katrina in 2005. The French colony of Louisiana, the basis of the modern State, was founded around 1700, and purchased by the US in 1803, after a period of Spanish rule. In 1730, its population was around seven thousand, of which two thousand were slaves.

18 The brevity and economy of Puccini's depiction of the death of Mimì in *La Bohème* are sometimes compared to this long drawn out scene which lasts eighteen minutes, and is full of sombre colours, scarcely leaving the minor key. It has been described as a dramatic blunder. Maybe Puccini had little choice: having concluded the Embarkation scene, he had to get the lovers away somewhere to die.

La Bohème

The 'Holy Trinity': Puccini with Giacosa and Illica,
the team for *La Bohème*, *Tosca* and *Madama Butterfly*.

Contents

La Bohème: Background

The image of 'Bohemians',[1] students and their *grisettes*[2] living in attics in the Latin Quarter of Paris, was established around 1850 by the writer Henry Mürger[3] whose series of sketches, 'Scènes de la vie de bohème', was based on his personal experience of bohemian life.

Mürger might have been lost to history had not Puccini half a century later transmuted him into Mimì's lover Rodolfo. *La Bohème* has remained one of the most popular operas. For many theatres, it is 'an old standby', which has been sung by all the star tenors and sopranos of Italian opera. There is a tendency for celebrities to regard themselves as the attraction rather than the opera, but arguably that is preferable to the focus being on the production itself.

Puccini created *La Bohème* with immense skill and artistry, using an unlikely and quarrelsome pair of librettists: one a former sailor, the rough, republican, quick-working Luigi Illica, who produced the structure and first draft; the other, the smoother socialite, the very highly regarded poet and playwright Giuseppe Giacosa, a perfectionist who painstakingly versified and polished it.

This 'holy trinity' (as the music publisher Giulio Ricordi called them – see pages 12 & 13) had been involved in Puccini's first big-hitting production, *Manon Lescaut*. After *La Bohème*, they went on to create *Tosca* and *Madama Butterfly*. Their stormy relationship was exacerbated when Illica suggested that versification was of no relevance in a libretto; Giacosa, on the other hand, was infuriated by Puccini's endless refinements and changes as the work progressed. At one stage, Giacosa threatened to pull out of the project. Shortly thereafter, it was Illica's turn to explode. 'Illica should calm down,' said Puccini. Acts 3 and 4 proved particularly intractable, and Giacosa again offered to disclaim responsibility and waive any remuneration.

---

1 The term 'Bohemian', used to describe anyone who sets social conventions aside, originated from a misconception that such people came from Bohemia (just as gypsies were supposedly from Egypt).
2 Grisettes were the working-class girls of Paris. Their background, denoted by the customary grey dress which they wore, enhanced their sexuality.
3 Henry Mürger (1822–1861) was born in Paris. His father was a concierge and a tailor. He started work in a lawyer's office, but, with the help of an influential literary patron, became secretary to a Russian count. His literary activity was unfruitful until the publication in 1848 of his collected sketches entitled *Vie de Bohème*. Thereafter, his life was easier. According to *Encyclopaedia Britannica*, his writings 'exhibit the same characteristics – an excellent descriptive faculty, lively humour in drawing the follies of youth, frequently pathos, and not seldom a tender and poetical melancholy'.

Toscanini conducted the première at the Teatro Regio in Turin on 1 February, 1896. This was the third anniversary of *Manon Lescaut*, and around seven weeks after Puccini had finished composing. The public liked the opera, but the critics were 'decidedly hostile' at first. The realism of the subject matter may have been too hard to swallow.

Puccini's initial feeling of mortification was premature. The production ran well and a subsequent performance in Palermo was prolonged by encores beyond 1am; by then, half the orchestra had left, the cast had changed out of most of their clothes, Rodolfo had removed his wig and Mimì's hair was all over the place. The conductor decided to repeat the whole of the last scene.

La Bohème became very popular indeed. People started calling their babies Mimì. King George V told the conductor Sir Thomas Beecham that it was his favourite opera, because it was the shortest one he knew. It is now at the top of 'the charts'. Indeed, before the time of the long-running, highly marketed West End musical, the number of performances of *La Bohème* was probably the highest ever attained by any serious stage work, including plays.

When Puccini was secretly working away on *La Bohème*, he discovered that his contemporary Ruggero Leoncavallo, the composer of *Pagliacci*, was also composing an opera based on the same sketches and its dramatised version. The two composers had a blazing row in a Milan café and this was followed by announcements in separate newspapers that each was working on the same opera. Puccini's blunt response was 'Let him compose. I shall compose, and the public will judge'. Leoncavallo's version was premièred fifteen months after Puccini's and, at first, was actually the more popular of the two.

Who's Who and What's What

This summary is based on the libretto. As mentioned in the Warning at the end of this book, certain directors may amend opera stories to suit their production.

It is Christmas time around 1830, in Paris. **Rodolfo**, a poet, **Marcello**, a painter, **Colline**, a philosopher, and **Schaunard**, a musician who is managing to make some money, live, in a rumbustious jolly male way, in a freezing garret. They are in arrears with their rent which their landlord **Benoît** comes unsuccessfully to collect. Rodolfo stays behind when the others go off to the Café Momus.

In total contrast, **Mimì**,[4] a frail and undernourished seamstress who lives next door, comes to obtain a light for her candle. We do not have to wait long for Rodolfo's *Che gelida manina* ('Your tiny hand is frozen') and her response *Mi chiamano Mimì* ('They call me Mimì ...'), followed by his *O soave fanciulla*.[5] Thus their love affair begins.

Marcello's ex-girlfriend **Musetta**, has left him for an elderly and rich protector, **Alcindoro**. But in a colourful scene at the **Café Momus** in the Latin Quarter, Musetta and Marcello come together again, having made the old man look an ass.

A few weeks later, in February, near the **Barrière d'Enfer**, a customs post on the walls, we hear that Mimì's romance with Rodolfo is not going so well, despite their love for each other. She is increasingly ill, suffering from consumption. She returns to the garret to die.

---

4 Whereas the tendency in English is to pronounce Mimì with the accent on the first syllable, it should be pronounced with the accent on the second. Where the rest of the cast finds the Mimì uncooperative, she has been known to be called 'Moomoo', a bovine imitation.
5 This is one of the best-known and best-loved sequences in Italian opera. English has no obvious words with which to translate the expression *O soave fanciulla* – 'Sweet young girl' is one approximation. Translating it 'sweet maiden', as is sometimes done, would seem technically incorrect for a poor worker in Paris in that era.

TALKING POINTS

Giacomo Puccini (1858–1924)
Please see the summary of the life of Puccini on pages 159 and 160.

Puccini's Place as a Composer – a View
The view expressed on pages 161-163 is very relevant.

The real Vie de Bohème
It was not until the 1850s and 1860s that the town planner and Prefect of the Seine, Baron Haussman, bulldozed the quaint and medieval Paris and created the city we know, with its broad boulevards. At the time in which *La Bohème* is set, the city was housing over forty percent more people than at the turn of the previous century. The migration into towns of country people in search of work created overwhelming strain on living and working conditions (thirty years later, nearly seventy percent of the population of Paris originated from elsewhere). By the mid-nineteenth century, only one in five buildings was connected to the public water supply. The tenements had collective lavatories, which were emptied by two thousand three hundred night-soil carts.

Economic desperation and the temptation of higher earnings drove girls such as Mimì and Musetta to prostitution, which was among the most common occupations for single, working-class women. Those not registered to work in the 180–200 licensed brothels lived in abject poverty or in the Saint-Lazare prison, which had separate divisions for under and over thirteen years of age. In Paris in 1846, thirteen percent of babies were abandoned.

The easygoing morality of the 'Vie de bohème' sketches was criticised at the time. Its apologists pointed out that Rodolphe (Rodolfo) is not presented as a hero, and the author does not disguise the folly of the bohemians.

Detail in the libretto
Puccini took immense interest in the choice and development of his librettos, which are surprisingly criticised for being too sparing with words. In *La Bohème*, the mixture of laughter and passion is highly effective, as is the use of contrast as a means of reinforcing the drama. For example, in act 3, the underlying true love of Mimì and Rodolfo is reinforced by its juxtaposition with the bickering of Musetta and

Marcello. And the entry of the dying Mimì during the mock-duel adds considerably to the dramatic effect.

Musetta, although second to Mimì, has a major role and is most effectively characterised. She may be a prostitute, through desperation, but is full of humanity. Her prayer while Mimì is dying in act 4 is wrenching, just as her bickering with Marcello and her treatment of her protector Alcindoro are totally realistic.

It has been suggested that 'where erotic passion, sensuality, tenderness, pathos and despair meet and fuse, Puccini was an unrivalled master'.

Detail in the music

Puccini, together with his rivals Leoncavallo and Mascagni, used Bizet's *Carmen* as a model. So, the music provides us with wonderfully colourful and realistic scenes, for example, the crowd scene at Café Momus in act 2, or dawn coming up over Paris at the beginning of act 3. Surprisingly, those parallel fifths on the flutes and harp, suggestive of a spooky dawn, were castigated by critics following the première.

In Rodolfo, Puccini provided a means for great singers to excel, and *Che gelida manina* is the role's greatest challenge. Pavarotti said that its quiet, low notes need a 'steady pure sound that floods the opera house'. Despite being soft, they require behind them all the power that the singer possesses: 'they need the same amount of support from the diaphragm that you give to the big notes'.

The orchestration, which infuses the drama, will be absorbed by most audiences subconsciously. Thus most listeners are unlikely to be aware just how subtle and unostentatious it is: Puccini's leading biographer described 'the astounding sleight of hand with which he manages an incessant interplay of action, characters and atmosphere'. But listen to the effective use of the harp throughout the opera, and perhaps particularly in act 3. Note also the slightly ponderous use of the woodwind to accompany the philosopher Colline as he sends off his coat to be pawned in act 4. Rodolfo and Mimì are chiefly accompanied by strings, Musetta by woodwind.

The score was painstakingly prepared. It is unusually detailed and is littered with instructions on dynamics (and everything else). Just before the final two bars of act 3, when Rodolfo and Mimì are reconciled, the dynamic is marked *ppppp*. There is no word for this unusual marking. It can be interesting to consider whether the conductor has realised the composer's intention and brought out the subtlety of this relative to other gradations of pianissimo, *pp*, *ppp*, and *pppp*. Puccini's response when

Ricordi, his publisher, remonstrated with him was: 'As for the *pp*'s and the *ff*'s of the score, if I have overdone them it is because, as Verdi says, when one wants piano, one puts *ppp*'.

Puccini completed *La Bohème* around midnight on 10 December, 1895. According to the mythology, his mates were playing cards next door, calling their hands and drinking. All this while Puccini was working away. Puccini then joined them for a binge and a shoot. Considering the painstaking detail and workmanship in the last few pages, this tale is hard to credit. The other tale, that when Puccini finished the last few notes he stood up and wept, is certainly credible – perhaps like the audience weeps when the curtain falls.

Consumption (tuberculosis or TB)

In the 1820s, almost half of all deaths in Paris were due to pulmonary consumption, pneumonia, pleurisy and intestinal complaints. The social disruption, and the prevalent social conditions of the time, were later immortalised in Victor Hugo's *Les Misérables*. Even in late nineteenth-century Europe, consumption was blamed for one-seventh of the death rate.

Chopin and Weber are the better-known examples of composers alleged to have suffered from consumption. It was a disease which was particularly prevalent among the poor, who suffered from bad nutrition, cramped conditions and lack of sanitation. The terrifying symptoms were coughing and blood-stained sputum. For years, there was a desperate attempt to find a cure. Even at the end of the nineteenth century, it was being suggested that long sea voyages, such as those to Australia or New Zealand, could be a means of arresting the disease.

Only in 1882 did the Nobel prize-winner Robert Koch (1843–1910) discover the bacillus that was the cause of the condition. And not until after the Second World War was immunisation widespread. The disease is still a significant cause of death worldwide.

ACT BY ACT

Puccini pointed out that the hardest thing is to decide how to begin an opera – 'how to find its musical atmosphere. Once the opening has been determined, there is nothing more to fear.' So it is not surprising that the music of *La Bohème* immediately grabs our attention and takes us straight into the Latin Quarter of Paris in the 1830s.

Act 1 Christmas, a garret in Paris

The garret is home to four impoverished 'artists': Rodolfo, a poet; Marcello, a painter; Colline, a philosopher; and Schaunard, a musician. It is Christmas Eve, freezing cold, and it has been snowing.

Marcello sits with Rodolfo. He is trying to paint a picture of the Red Sea, but it is too cold: it is as cold, he opines, as his girlfriend Musetta's heart. Rodolfo looks longingly out over the rooftops at the smoke emanating from the chimneys. Desperate for some warmth, they contemplate breaking up the furniture for the fire; instead, Rodolfo sacrifices the manuscript of his latest play, all three acts, one after the other. Colline, the philosopher, returns having tried unsuccessfully to pawn some of his books.

The fire is about finally to flicker out when they are all astonished to see Schaunard, the musician, coming in with food and money. While the others try to relight the fire, he explains that an eccentric Englishman employed him as a musician to play for three days. Besides which, he also succeeded in seducing the maid.

The others lay the table with a newspaper as tablecloth. But Schaunard insists that the food should be put in the larder. As it is Christmas Eve, they should dine out. They decide to have a drink first.

At this moment, Benoît the landlord, who is owed three months' rent, bangs on the door with his demand. They reluctantly invite him in. They get him drunk. They talk about chasing girls and he recounts his conquests. But when he admits to having a wife, they feign moral indignation and kick him out.

When they leave for the café, Rodolfo stays behind for five minutes to finish an article for a journal, 'The Beaver'.[6]

---

6 *Le Castor* ('The Beaver') was the name of a journal in which Mürger, the author of *Vie de Bohème*, wrote.

Rodolfo cannot work up any inspiration. He hears a knock at the door. A frail, pale and consumptive girl enters in a state of near-collapse, and explains that her candle has gone out.[7] She faints, dropping her candle and key. He revives her with a drink. She says it was just the effort of climbing the stairs. She asks him to relight the candle and makes to go. Then she remembers that she has forgotten her key. As she comes back in, the wind blows both candles out. In the moonlight, they try to find the key. When Rodolfo comes across it, he puts it in his pocket.

As they continue to search in the darkness, their hands touch: *Che gelida manina, se la lasci riscaldar,*[8] in which great tenors linger on the high Cs. In this, perhaps the most famous sequence in all opera, Rodolfo tells her that he is a poet. She replies that her name is Lucia, but they call her Mimì: *Mi chiamano Mimì.*[9] She is a seamstress, who embroiders silk and satin with flowers which, of course, have no perfume. She lives alone in the next-door room.

The others wonder why Rodolfo is taking so long, and they call out for him. He tells them to go on to Café Momus and keep a table. In the moonlight, Rodolfo is overwhelmed with Mimì's beauty – *O soave fanciulla*. There are now just the two of them, and they sing the famous duet, with its theme that is to be associated with Mimì. They kiss – at first she resists, but soon she abandons herself to passion – the score is marked *Con abbandono*. She reaches top C, and he, if not in unison, reaches top E: *Amor!* Puccini was never to surpass the delicate poetry of this love scene.

Act 2 Later, in the Latin Quarter

Puccini depicts a colourful crowd scene in the street outside Café Momus, which is doing a brisk trade. Street vendors call their wares and the urchins, students and others mill around. Schaunard tries a horn; Rodolfo buys Mimì a bonnet; Colline is after a frockcoat and then a runic grammar; Marcello just wants a woman. The mothers drag their children away from the itinerant toy seller.

---

7 Opera operates on the brink of the absurd, as the stout coloratura soprano who sings the role of the consumptive Mimì often illustrates.

8 Caruso, who did not like Melba, is said to have placed a hot potato (or, some say, a sausage) in her hand at this moment when she was playing Mimì to his Rodolpho. Pavarotti subsequently took a dim view of this: 'To me it seems very unprofessional,' he wrote. In another staging, in a freezing theatre during the Second World War, when Rodolfo sang 'Your tiny hand is frozen,' she whispered, 'You're telling Mimì'.

9 Puccini is very precise in his requirements. The score abounds with his instructions: for example, when Mimì describes 'the first kiss' of spring, she is instructed to sing *Con grande espansione*, and *Con espressione intense*, indicating broadening out, and great emotional intensity. Such expressions are well beyond the routine ones found in general glossaries of musical terms.

The friends order supper and Rodolfo introduces Mimì. They enjoy their meal and the jollifications.

Musetta, Marcello's former girlfriend enters, expensively attired, with an elderly protector, Alcindoro de Mitonneaux, in tow. People think Musetta is beautiful – and she knows it. In the street, all eyes are on her: *Quando me'n vo soletta per la via*.[10] She treats Alcindoro like a dog and calls him 'Lulu', a name he wishes she would reserve for intimacies. The crowd sees the opportunity to fleece him.

Musetta has only recently split up from Marcello, who is deeply upset with her because she is like a weather-vane. To her annoyance, Marcello ignores her, so she throws a plate on the ground to draw attention to herself.

Musetta, who is really the star of act 2, pretends to be addressing Alcindoro while in fact she is addressing Marcello. She pretends her shoe is hurting her and orders Alcindoro to run quickly to the cobbler: *Corri va corri! Presto, va, va!* Musetta and Marcello embrace. When the waiter brings the bill, they have run out of cash, but Musetta gets him to add their bill to Alcindoro's. Some soldiers on patrol march along, led by their drum-major. They all joyfully parade off with the soldiers, leaving the exasperated Alcindoro, who has returned from the cobbler, to pick up the two bills presented to him by the waiter. [11]

Act 3 February, next to the Barrière d'Enfer, a customs post on the walls of Paris

It is February. Snow falls. Paris is waking up, and street-sweepers, milkmaids and peasants arrive through one of the Paris Barrières, or city gates, next to an inn sign painted by Marcello.

Mimì, distressed and coughing, comes searching for Marcello, who is lodging at the inn with Musetta (she teaches singing to the patrons, while he is painting signboards).

Mimì (reaching high B flat) asks for help with her relationship with Rodolfo, who is so jealous and possessive. Marcello suggests that Mimì and Rodolfo should split up. She hides when Rodolfo appears. Rodolfo

---

10 Puccini got the idea for Musetta's waltz when he was out shooting in his boat, which was gently rocked by the waves.
11 Opera-goers attending *La Bohème* at Covent Garden in May 2012 were dismayed to be told that the performance would be interrupted so that a TV station could film a celebrity attempting to conduct a rerun of act 2. Opera-goers are increasingly used to productions which show little fidelity to the composer's intentions. Lengthy interruptions are however a new and disrespectful development. Puccini intended his opera to be performed as a single uninterrupted work (the story is, after all, very dramatic). Top performers might be allowed a bow, and an occasional encore.

criticises Mimì as a *civetta* – a coquette – who shows off her ankle to every dandy viscount. But he loves her. However, his freezing garret is totally unsuitable for someone as ill as her, and he is so frightened for her. Mimì overhears this and is horrified.

Mimì's coughing reveals her hiding place. Marcello hears Musetta flirting and rushes into the inn. Mimì tells Rodolfo that they must part, although without bitterness: *Addio senza rancor* (Puccini at first thickens her sound with a solo clarinet an octave below). She will return to her small room where she dreamt of spring. He should arrange for her possessions to be returned to her, but he may keep the pink bonnet as a souvenir. Ironically, while they sing poetically of love, their dreams and morning-rise – *Addio, dolce svegliar* – Musetta and Marcello have a rip-roaring row about her flirting. Mimì and Rodolfo are reconciled, to the sound of a solo violin, an octave above.

Act 4 The garret in Paris
The orchestra takes us straight back to the original garret, where Marcello and Rodolfo pretend to work, but talk of Musetta and Mimì. Schaunard and Colline appear with some bread and a herring. They fool around and pretend to have a feast and a ball. They drown their sorrows. Colline and Schaunard have a mock duel. [12]

Their antics are suddenly interrupted by Musetta. She says that Mimì is climbing slowly up the stairs, and is very ill. Musetta had heard that Mimì had left her protector, the viscount that she had taken up with, and she came across her in the street. There is nothing left to eat or drink in the garret. Mimì is frozen and coughing. Schaunard fears she will be dead in half an hour. Rodolfo tells her not to talk but to rest.

Musetta rips off her earrings and tells the others to pawn them and fetch a doctor. She goes to get a muff, which Mimì craves. Colline sadly, but generously, gives his old coat over to be pawned, with the music providing the right tone for the dénouement.

They sense that it is time to leave Rodolfo and Mimì to each other. [13]

---

12 The props in this scene can create problems. A stage hand, who was asked to provide a herring, forgot that he was boiling a fish on the stage doorkeeper's gas ring and over-cooked it. When thrown around, the fish disintegrated, and showered the singers with powder. Likewise, an old cushion that Schaunard used to fend off Colline disintegrated when struck with the poker.

13 Away from an audience, the company can be allowed some fun. In rehearsal, Sir Thomas Beecham once called for more volume from his dying Mimì. 'Don't you realise that it is difficult to sing lying down?' she asked. Beecham replied, 'I seem to recollect that I have given some of my best performances in that position.'

Mimì pretends to be asleep so that she can be alone with Rodolfo: *Sono andati? Fingevo di dormire*. They have so much to talk about. (This has been described as 'sadness incarnate' and 'one of the most inspired melodies that ever sprang into Puccini's head.')

The musical themes of the earlier acts recur. The lovers recall their first meeting and how they held hands together in the dark: we hear echoes of *Che gelida manina*. Rodolfo shows Mimì the bonnet, the souvenir. She is convulsed with a spasm, coughing. Marcello and Musetta return with the muff and a cordial; they say that the doctor is coming. Musetta gives Mimì the muff and pretends it is from Rodolfo.

Mimì sinks and fades away. Musetta heats the cordial and prays. The others know what has happened. Eventually, it dawns on Rodolfo that Mimì is dead.

Tosca

The 'Holy Trinity': Puccini with Giacosa and Illica,
the team for *La Bohème*, *Tosca* and *Madama Butterfly*.

Contents

Tosca: Background

Today, it is hopefully unusual for a terrorist threat to disrupt an opera première. On 14 January, 1900, it was less so. In recent years, bombs had gone off in theatres in Barcelona and Pisa.

The Queen and members of the Government were expected for the first night of *Tosca* at Rome's Constanzi Theatre. There had been a rumour of an attack. Indeed, the conductor Leopoldo Mugnone,[1] who had himself experienced the Barcelona incident, was told to play the national anthem if there should be one. He did not. The noise of latecomers during the start so worried him that he left the podium soon after the curtain went up. Fortunately, it was only a hoax, and the performance resumed.

Puccini's opera is based on Sardou's 'blood and thunder' melodrama *La Tosca* (1884), which was written for the great actress Sarah Bernhardt. Although the sadism and brutality in Puccini's opera was frowned upon at the time – the critics gave it a rather lukewarm reception – it quickly became an outstanding success. The public flocked to it then, and have ever since. It is not often one gets, in one evening, torture, an attempted rape, a murder, an execution and two suicides; and a police chief fantasising during a 'Te Deum' in a church. It is not surprising that it has attracted more than its fair share of mirth.

Puccini had thought of making use of Sardou's play ten years before his *Tosca* première. He was prompted to return to it, largely because of the vogue for 'realism': Mascagni's *Cavalleria rusticana* had been a great success ten years before, as had Leoncavallo's *Pagliacci* subsequently. And the play would make a good opera. Verdi had indicated that, had he been younger, he would have been interested in using it.

The right to turn it into an opera had been given to another composer, Franchetti. But, with utter knavery and dishonesty, Puccini's publisher Giulio Ricordi (see pages 12 & 13) persuaded him that it was a totally unsuitable subject, so he relinquished his rights. Ricordi immediately signed up Puccini.

---

1 Mugnone was the distinguished conductor of several premières, including *Cavalleria rusticana*. Beecham thought him the best Italian conductor of his time.

Victorien Sardou (1831–1908), a loquacious raconteur – Puccini found it difficult to get a word in edgeways – was a very successful French dramatist in the second half of the nineteenth century. His output of more than seventy plays has attracted mixed views: the music critic and dramatist George Bernard Shaw considered them lightweight, and invented the term 'Sardoudledom' to characterise them. A leading twentieth-century authority on Puccini has described the ingredients of Sardou's *La Tosca* as 'sex, sadism, religion and art, mixed by a master-chef with the whole dish served on the platter of an important historical event'.

Sardou recommended 'torturing the women' as an important ingredient of a successful play. There are four corpses in *Tosca*, and Puccini suggested to his publisher that perhaps Sardou, who was known as 'the Caligula of the theatre', would insist on killing Spoletta too.

The opera took Puccini three years to compose. He collaborated with Luigi Illica and Giuseppe Giacosa, in the improbable and quarrelsome team (the 'holy trinity') which also created *La Bohème* and *Madama Butterfly*. Illica, who was a rough republican, and who connived in the deception of Franchetti, produced the structure and first draft. Giacosa, the playwright, a calmer character, versified and polished it, despite at first thinking that Sardou's play was very unsuitable, being 'a drama of coarse emotional situations ... all plot and no poetry'. In his view, Sardou's final act was 'one interminable duet.' Even when Puccini had finished, Ricordi panicked about the third act and Puccini had to calm him down.

It has been rightly suggested that 'where erotic passion, sensuality, tenderness, pathos and despair meet and fuse, Puccini was an unrivalled master'. Perhaps because *Tosca* is as explicit and exciting as a piece of good television, with many of the same ingredients, it has been produced as a self-standing film several times.

Puccini demonstrates an extraordinary sense of theatre: the conclusion of act 1, the Te Deum scene with its procession and chorus, has been 'reckoned one of the most impressive finali in all opera'. There are lesser details: each act begins with an attention-grabbing orchestral phrase: you must put aside your glass of wine! And each act ends with a spine-chilling, devastating declaration: *Tosca, mi fai dimenticare Iddio!* ('Tosca, you make me forget God'); *E avanti a lui tremava tutta Roma!* ('All Rome trembled before him'); *O Scarpia, avanti a Dio!* ('Scarpia, let's meet before God!')[2]

As well as being profoundly moved, we can leave the theatre humming one of those incandescent lyrical phrases, brief, simple and thus so memorable, from arias such as *Vissi d'arte, E lucevan le stelle* and *O dolci mani.*

Tosca is surely secure in its place in the top ten operas.

---

2 Callas told a pupil 'You must give the public the shivers'. Enormous effort goes into making the production effective. For the Callas recording, Tito Gobbi had to sing his act 1 music thirty times, working on colour and inflection even in individual syllables; and she worked on the phrase *E avanti a lui tremava tutta Roma* for half an hour. For Domingo's film, the filming of the first-act duet between Tosca and Cavaradossi took nineteen hours, from noon till 7am.

WHO'S WHO AND WHAT'S WHAT

This summary is based on the libretto. As mentioned in the Warning at the end of this book, certain directors may amend opera stories to suit their production.

Most unusually for opera, the action is set on a specific day at a specific time. It takes place in Rome, during sixteen hours overnight on 14 June, 1800.

Cesare Angelotti, a high-profile political prisoner on the run, rushes into a church, seeking sanctuary. The **sacristan** has been cleaning brushes for the artist **Mario Cavaradossi**, who is painting a portrait of Mary Magdalen. **Floria Tosca**, herself a prima donna, is in love with Cavaradossi and is rightly extremely jealous and suspicious of the 'lady' he has depicted in the painting. He explains that art blends contrasting beauties: *Recondita armonia*.

By helping Angelotti's escape, Cavaradossi becomes implicated, and falls into the clutches of **Baron Scarpia**, the police chief, who is on the scent of the fugitive. Scarpia fancies Tosca. In the **Te Deum scene**, to the background of the religious ceremony, he relishes catching the prisoner and having the woman: for him, the rope, for her, bed: *Va, Tosca!*

He orders his henchman, the police agent **Spoletta**, to find, arrest and torture Cavaradossi. Angelotti is found and commits suicide. The sound of the preparations for the execution of Cavaradossi is too much for Tosca, who has lived for art and for love, as she explains in one of the most famous arias in opera: *Vissi d'arte, Vissi d'amore*. She barters her body for her lover's life. However, Scarpia explains that there will have to be a mock execution, and he writes a pardon and a passport to enable her and Cavaradossi to escape after this. She then stabs him when he moves forward to rape her.

Before dawn at the Castel Sant'Angelo, a **shepherd boy** passes with his flock, and various church bells chime. With one hour left before the **execution**, Cavaradossi bribes the **jailer** in return for permission to write a letter to Tosca. At the moment of death, he has never been so much in love: *E lucevan le stelle*. Tosca arrives with the pardon and passport. Cavaradossi is amazed when he hears what she did with her sweet hands: *O dolci mani*.

Cavaradossi is brought out for what Tosca expects is to be a mock execution. But Scarpia has played this trick successfully before: the execution is real. After Cavaradossi is shot, and Tosca discovers the truth, she leaps over the battlements.

As well as a chorus of clergy, soldiers and so on, other members of the cast include a torturer, a judge and **Sciarrone**, a gendarme.

Callas and Gobbi

TALKING POINTS

Giacomo Puccini (1858–1924)
Please see the summary of the life of Puccini on pages 159 and 160.

Puccini's Place as a Composer – a View
The view expressed on pages 161-163 is very relevant.

Italy in 1900, at the time of Tosca
Italy was politically unstable following its unification, which was only finally completed in 1871. The country comprised an uneasy amalgam of the industrial north and the feudal south, with the middle of the country predominantly agricultural. Political shenanigans were rife, involving sordid bargains between local interests, and promises of virtually anything if it would secure a parliamentary vote. There was a colonial failure in Ethiopia. A demonstration in Milan resulted in a massacre. Seven months after the *Tosca* première, King Umberto, who had survived various assassination threats and attempts, was finally shot by an Italian-American.

Tosca: the historical background
Like many dramatists, Sardou manipulated history and his characters to create an 'illusion of authenticity that still deceives many commentators'. The setting is an amalgam of the Roman and Neapolitan ('Parthenopean') Republics, two out of a series of short-lived constitutions which followed Napoleon's invasion of Italy in 1796.

The Republics were excessively revolutionary or just ineffective, and were largely a front for the French, whose domination was resented. An anti-revolutionary alliance of Crown, Church and peasantry overthrew them. There were fearful reprisals. Nelson, with his mistress Lady Hamilton, played a significant and far from creditable role in suppressing the Parthenopean Republic.

In Rome, Papal rule, as symbolised in *Tosca* by Scarpia, was restored. However, on 14 June, 1800, the specific date of *Tosca*, Rome, far from being tyrannised by a Scarpia, was actually lawless and chaotic.

The battle of Marengo took place that day. In a lightning campaign in May–June 1800, Napoleon, who by then was First Consul of France and keen to build on his position, crossed the Alps. He got behind the Austrians, who for years had dominated northern Italy. He was attacked by them on 14 June at Marengo, near to Turin. The battle went badly for Napoleon at first – hence the news in act 1 of *Tosca* – but in the afternoon the French recovered the position and won, as we hear in act 2. There were no mobiles in those days.

The victory was fortunate for Napoleon, whose position in Paris would have been severely weakened had he lost at Marengo. He in fact strengthened his image of 'statesmanship' by not reinstating the Roman and Parthenopean Republics. Later, when he became Emperor he distributed kingdoms in Italy to his relatives and supporters. His young son was created King of Rome, while the Papal States continued to be ruled by the subservient Pope.

Puccini's attention to detail: the music and the score

It is beyond doubt that Puccini was a consummate craftsman.

This is seen in the musical characterisation of the cast, the atmosphere, and the changes of mood on stage. In an attempt to follow Wagner, he uses around sixty musical labels for situations and objects. But *Tosca* is 'musical drama', not Wagnerian music drama. This may account for its immortality.

Puccini's scores were painstakingly prepared. The audience is not expected to pick up the detail, but, for example, in the last minute of act 2, following the stabbing of Scarpia, the cellos and basses are, within just six bars, instructed to play *con passione, con anima* and *col canto*. A few moments later the strings are told to play *il più piano possibile*, 'as quiet as possible' against a gong playing *ppp* and the bass drum *pppp*. A few bars later, the instruction *trattenuto* (holding back) precedes a *ritardando* (slowing up), and this is followed by *lontanissimi* (fading away) on the side drum. It can be interesting to consider whether the conductor has realised the composer's intention, and brought out these subtle gradations.

An opera for stars

In *Tosca*, Puccini has provided a means for great singers to star. Enrico Caruso was a famous Cavaradossi. Maria Callas, like her rival Renata Tebaldi, was a great Tosca;[3] Tito Gobbi was a memorable Scarpia. In films, producers such as Franco Zeffirelli created an unforgettable dramatic experience.

Audiences used to conventional grand divas in massive robes, walking sticks, gloves and feathered hats were captivated by Callas's sensuality and sexuality. At one moment, she could be torn with jealousy; in the next, she could also plumb new depths of tenderness. She 'revealed depths in the role that few suspected were there.' She made the *Vissi d'arte* into

---

3 The first record Callas's mother bought her was of the *Vissi d'arte*.

an integral part of the musical drama, not just the showpiece about which Puccini himself felt uncomfortable, because he worried that it delayed the forward drive of the action.

Maria Jeritza, the acclaimed Czech soprano, said that the part of Tosca is far more taxing dramatically than vocally.

The physical requirements for males are rather different. In one production, Pavarotti was expected to be up on scaffolding painting a vast canvas. There was a logistical problem: how to get him down to perform the love duet with Tosca. (For Pavarotti, the problem was medical: he had a bad knee.) So the producer arranged for him to be on the ground painting a sketch of the much larger painting which was up on the easel. Pavarotti observed 'Sometimes you must remind designers and directors they are working with human beings, not acrobats'.

Jinxed?
Because *Tosca* is so dramatic and effective,[4] it has attracted ribald mirth and has facilitated more legends than other operas.

The firing squad is known to have 'shot' Tosca rather than Cavaradossi – much to the confusion of the unrehearsed soldiers, who, having been told to exit with the principals, all leapt over the battlements after Tosca. And Tosca has been known to mistakenly kick a pile of cannonballs on the battlements; being rubber balls painted black, they bounced slowly down into the orchestra pit and stalls.

The highly dramatic scene at the end of act 2 lends itself to things going wrong, because of the candles. Tosca has been known to set fire to Scarpia's wig. Callas's wig also caught fire. Galina Vishnevskaya leant back against the table just before stabbing Scarpia and her wig touched one of the candles. She was surprised that instead of falling down dead, he went for her hair. He pulled off her wig, and Placido Domingo, who tells the story, and was waiting in the wings, doused it with the 'wine'.

Less seriously, a Scarpia found his trousers falling down, perhaps conveniently, when chasing Tosca around. Earlier in the scene, at the cry of 'Vittoria', Domingo flung his head back and broke the nose of a supernumerary behind him.

Maria Jeritza walked towards the sofa where she was supposed to sing

---

4 The reader can decide whether to be as enthusiastic as Gustav Kobbé who considered that Scarpia's death is 'a wonderful scene – one of the greatest in all drama.'

the *Vissi d'arte*. She slipped and sang from a prone position. Puccini had said that that is how it was to be sung; that is, Tosca should address her aria not to Scarpia, but to heaven. On another occasion, she stabbed with such violence that the knife penetrated Scarpia's Empire coat, waistcoat and silk shirt, and grazed the skin. After that, she was always required to use a leather dagger.

Callas: a leather knife too?

ACT BY ACT

Act 1 The Church of Sant' Andrea della Valle

The opera opens in the church, where an easel with a large painting indicates that an artist has been at work. The scene is set with three ferocious chords, played as loud as the orchestra can. These, and the 'whole tone' scale on which they are based, are later to be associated with the sinister character of the police chief. A fugitive rushes in. He finds a key at the base of a statue of the Madonna, and quickly lets himself into a side chapel belonging to the Attavanti family.

The comic sacristan wanders in with the artist's brushes, which he has been cleaning; he prays as soon as the Angelus sounds. Mario Cavaradossi appears and reveals his painting, a portrait of a beautiful Magdalen. The sacristan observes that it is modelled on a blonde blue-eyed girl who comes regularly to pray and leave a basket of provisions. Cavaradossi compares the face on a locket with that in the painting. He reassures himself that when he is painting the Magdalen, his mind is actually thinking of the dark, black-eyed Floria Tosca, the celebrated singer: art blends contrasting beauties, *Recondita armonia*. His sentiments shock the sacristan who asks to be excused, but has his eye on the basket of food.

The fugitive emerges from his hiding place. Cavaradossi recognises him as Cesare Angelotti, formerly a Consul of the Roman Republic, and for a long time incarcerated in the Castel Sant'Angelo.

When Tosca is heard arriving, Cavaradossi tells the jailbird to hide and gives him the food. Tosca sees the picture and jealously concludes that Cavardossi loves the blonde woman. When he tries to kiss her, she protests that they should not do it in front of a statue of the Madonna. She arranges to meet him after her concert performance that evening. They can make love by the light of the full moon in his villa in the woods. She upbraids him for not being enthusiastic enough, and describes the romantic nature of their trysting place.

Cavardossi really wants to get on with his painting, but Tosca continues to take exception to the picture. She recognises that the model for the Magdalen is a member of the Attavanti family. She is annoyed by the eyes and, before leaving, insists that he should paint them black like hers.

As soon as she is gone, Angelotti emerges again and explains that his sister has hidden some clothes for him to use as a disguise. Cavaradossi now understands why the woman used to come to pray so fervently: it was the love of a sister. They describe the evil nature of the vicious, but ostensibly pious, chief of police, Baron Scarpia. Cavaradossi tells

46

Angelotti to get out through the chapel to his villa and, if necessary, hide in the well. He will accompany him.

To celebrate a defeat of Napoleon, the sacristan says that there is going to be a Te Deum, and that evening Tosca will sing at a gala concert at the Palazzo Farnese.

A gun sounds, indicating that the prisoner's escape has been discovered. At this moment, there is a hush: the fearsome Scarpia, who has designs on Tosca, arrives with Spoletta, his police agent, in search of the prisoner. He discovers a fan and the basket, notices the Attavanti coat of arms on the fan, and the lady in the picture. When told by the sacristan that Cavaradossi painted it, Scarpia concludes that he, Tosca's lover, must have assisted the escaper. When Tosca herself returns, Scarpia knows that, just as Iago used a handkerchief (to deceive Othello), he can use the fan to trap Tosca into revealing the whereabouts of his prey.

First, Scarpia conceals himself behind a pillar. Tosca has returned to tell Cavaradossi that on account of the forthcoming gala they cannot have their tryst. She is surprised to find that Cavaradossi has gone.

Scarpia approaches her, *Tosca Divina*. With the fan, he taunts her that the Marchioness of Attavanti, the lady in the painting, is Cavaradossi's lover. At this, Tosca vows revenge: the Marchioness shall not have Cavaradossi tonight. Scarpia, feigning to be shocked at such thoughts being given expression in a church, tells his henchman to follow her. As the procession sings the Te Deum for the supposed victory over the armies of Napoleon, Scarpia relishes catching the prisoner and seducing the woman: for him, the rope, for her, bed: *Va, Tosca* ('Go Tosca, there is room in your heart for Scarpia'). He concludes dramatically, *Tosca, mi fai dimenticare Iddio* ('Tosca, you make me forget God').

Act 2 The Farnese Palace
At supper in his apartment, Scarpia reckons that, with Tosca as his bird of prey, both Cavaradossi and Angelotti will have been caught and despatched by dawn. The sound of the gala performance in honour of the Austrian victory can be heard in the background. Scarpia muses on his personal preference for sadistic conquest rather than tender courtship.

His henchman Spoletta reports that they followed Tosca to a cottage. They picked up a defiant Cavaradossi but lost Angelotti. Cavaradossi is brought in and refuses to admit any complicity. The gala, now with Tosca performing, continues in the background. Scarpia demands to know the whereabouts of Angelotti.

Tosca rushes in, in time to hear Cavaradossi being tortured in an adjacent chamber. Despite the blood spurting at every twist of an iron ring on his head, Cavaradossi refuses to answer, and orders Tosca not to do so. But the horrified Tosca eventually reveals that Angelotti is in the well. Cavaradossi is brought in. He is in a state of collapse[5] and reproaches Tosca for submitting.

The news that Napoleon has actually won, and not lost, the battle (of Marengo) is announced. Cavaradossi shouts 'Vittoria' in Scarpia's face, but is sent off to be hanged.

Tosca is left with Scarpia, who sits down to supper. She asks him his price to save Cavaradossi: *Quanto?* The police chief has been aroused by her behaviour, and her loathing just increases his determination to have her. The march to the scaffold is heard, and Scarpia says that preparations for the execution are in hand.

In one of the best-known arias, in which she reaches top B flat, the forlorn Tosca sings 'I lived for art. I lived for love': *Vissi d'arte, Vissi d'amore.* She tried to be religious; why has the Lord repaid her in this ghastly way? Spoletta returns and announces that Angelotti killed himself when they found him in the well.

Tosca submits to Scarpia's demand for her, but insists on assurance and a safe conduct for herself and Cavaradossi, on the road to Civitavecchia.[6] Scarpia says that it will be necessary to have a sham execution and gives an order for Cavaradossi to be shot, significantly, 'as they did with Count Palmieri'. While Scarpia is writing out[7] the safe conduct, Tosca gets hold of a knife from the table. As he gives her the safe conduct, he lurches forward to take her: *Tosca, finalmente mia!* ('Tosca, at last you are mine!'). *Questo è il bacio di Tosca!* ('That is Tosca's kiss!') she replies as she drives the knife into him.

---

5 This moment of drama is prone to disaster. Pavarotti was reassured by the director that the antique stool on which he was expected to collapse had been reinforced with steel. On the night, the Tosca was so involved that, instead of rushing to embrace him, she landed on top. The stool caved in, to the dismay of cast and stage management; fortunately the audience thought that the mid-stage heap was intentional. Occasionally a Cavaradossi has been so enraged by Scarpia's sadism that he has gone for him. One, Tito Schipa, had to be restrained by Spoletta from attacking him: 'Hold him down,' the Scarpia yelled.
6 Civitavecchia is around fifty miles from Rome, for which it has long been the main port.
7 Some Scarpias take this opportunity to write messages. Sigurd Björling once wrote to Birgit Nilsson, 'Today you are, if that is possible, better than ever. Your Scarpia', making it rather difficult for her to continue loathing him.

While he suffocates in his own blood, she taunts him. All Rome trembled before him! *E avanti a lui tremava tutta Roma!*

She calmly tidies herself, and takes two candles from the table and puts one on either side of Scarpia's dead body. She takes a crucifix from the wall and places it on his breast. She goes out and shuts the door.

Act 3 Castel Sant'Angelo

It is before 4am. A shepherd boy passes with his flock, and various church bells call matins. Cavaradossi, under escort, is brought up to the platform on the ramparts. He gives the jailer his ring in return for his last wish: to write a letter. At the moment that he must die, his mind is on Tosca: he has never been so much in love. The orchestra depicts his thought processes, which he himself expresses in the famous, 'emotionally charged' aria, *E lucevan le stelle* ('When the stars were shining brightly').[8]

Spoletta brings Tosca, who has come with the safe conduct. She tells Cavaradossi about Scarpia's demise, reaching top C in the process. He is amazed that she killed him with her sweet hands: *O dolci mani.* She explains that there is to be a mock execution. After this, they will escape to Civitavecchia, where a ship awaits them. They sing of love and freedom; reaching top B, she tells him he must act the part very realistically, as she would on stage, and lie still until she calls him.

The bell sounds 4am. The firing squad prepares. Tosca is nervous. The soldiers fire. Spoletta stops the sergeant from delivering the coup de grace. While the squad departs, she worries that Cavaradossi will move. Then, leaning over the body, she is horrified to find that he is actually dead.

People are heard below shouting: Scarpia's murder has been discovered. Spoletta roars that she will pay for his life. She retorts 'with my own', as she shoves him away. She hurls herself over the battlements, crying *O Scarpia, avanti a Dio!* ('Scarpia! Let's meet before God!').[9]

---

8 Puccini was virtually wholly responsible for this famous aria, 'for composing the music, for causing the words to be written, and for declining expert advice from his librettists to throw the result into the waste-paper basket'.

9 This is the famous moment when the fat soprano has been known to bounce on the mattress and reappear above the battlements several times. One soprano was so disliked that the New York stage crew deliberately substituted a trampoline in the place of the mattress, thus ensuring fifteen bounces in various positions. There have been more serious health and safety issues: Kiri Te Kanawa badly hurt her back when making the leap.

Madama Butterfly

The 'Holy Trinity': Puccini with Giacosa and Illica,
the team for *La Bohème*, *Tosca* and *Madama Butterfly*.

CONTENTS

MADAMA BUTTERFLY: BACKGROUND

Early in Puccini's opera, we hear that Cio-Cio-San is called 'Madama or Madame Butterfly' because she possesses all the delicacy, lightness and transparency of the fluttering tiny creature. In her early years, Maria Callas was invited to sing the part for her début at the Metropolitan Opera. To everybody's amazement, she turned the opportunity down: she reckoned that, weighing in at nearly thirteen stone, it would not work. How wise she was.

Much later, when a slimmer Callas sang in Chicago, a member of the audience commented 'I never want to hear her Butterfly again. I'll end up liking this dreadful opera'. We can wonder whether it was Butterfly, the geisha,[1] which the individual did not like, or whether he was offended by Puccini's subtle portrayal of the arrogant cultural superiority assumed by 'the West'. It is surely amazing that music which quotes several times, and most disrespectfully, 'The Star-spangled Banner', can be found at the very top of lists of much-loved and most popular operas in the USA.

The libretto of *Madama Butterfly* is based on a story, almost certainly a true one, published in an 1898 magazine. The author was a Philadelphia lawyer, John Luther Long. The Far East had opened up to Western trade in the second half of the nineteenth century. Japan was now topical, sufficiently so for Gilbert & Sullivan to produce their operetta *The Mikado* in the mid-1880s.[2]

Puccini, who was most careful in his choice of opera libretti, had for some time been searching for a suitable subject to follow *Tosca*. He had even had a serious look at the possibilities of Victor Hugo's novel *Les Misérables* but rejected the idea. A one-act stage version of Long's story, by David Belasco,[3] was seen by the stage manager of Covent Garden who suggested that Puccini should come and see it. Thereafter, the negotiations with Belasco took nine months.

1 Geishas are traditional entertainers performing various Japanese arts, such as music and dance. The confusion with prostitutes particularly arises from the use of the term 'geisha girls' by American soldiers during the Occupation of Japan after the Second World War. Prostitutes wear the bow of the sash in front of their kimono whereas geishas wear it at the back. During the nineteenth century, there was a curious custom whereby visiting foreign naval officers were permitted to enter into temporary marriages with geishas, an arrangement which would terminate when the period of leave was up.

2 In 1868, the Emperor or 'Mikado' was reinstated as supreme authority in Japan. For six hundred and fifty years, real power had been vested in the Shogun, a military dictator, who operated from modern-day Tokyo, and the Mikado, who was housed in Kyoto, held a largely titular position.

3 David Belasco (1853–1931) was born in San Francisco, of Jewish origin. At first a clown, he became an actor, prolific writer, director, producer, and impresario. Puccini later used his *The Girl of the Golden West* for *La Fanciulla del West*.

Luigi Illica, who was a rough republican, produced the structure and first draft of the libretto; Giuseppe Giacosa, a calmer character, versified and polished it. This improbable and quarrelsome team, the 'holy trinity' (as the music publisher Giulio Ricordi called them), had also created Puccini's *Manon Lescaut*, *La Bohème* and *Tosca* (see pages 12 & 13).

The première of *Madama Butterfly* took place at La Scala on 17 February, 1904. Rosina Storchio was Cio-Cio-San, Giovanni Zenatello was Pinkerton, and Giuseppe de Luca was Sharpless. Puccini was very confident of its success. But complete pandemonium broke out in what was to be one of the sensational failures in the history of opera. Puccini withdrew it and revised it. He cut some of the material dealing with the wedding in act 1, and also provided for an interval, which some today regard as a mistake, between the night and the dawn in act 2.

Three months after the première, a revised version was staged with great success at the Teatro Grande in Brescia, a large city between Milan and Lake Garda. This was received with tremendous acclaim: *Un bel dì*, the letter scene, the flower scenes, and the Humming Chorus were encored; Puccini was called ten times. The opera has been a triumph ever since.

Puccini was more familiar than any of his contemporaries with the secrets of theatrical effect and success, such as the use of dramatic irony, where the audience knows what is going to happen, but the characters on stage, such as Madame Butterfly herself, do not.

The ultimate test of Puccini's achievement is surely this. The simple, almost naïve story of the gullible Japanese geisha singer is transformed by his use of music into an opera of tear-jerking emotion and intensity.

Musicologists cite his use of actual Japanese themes, and his use of exotic tone colour in the orchestra – woodwind, bells and gongs – to invent his own themes exhibiting 'the character which Japanese music has for Western ears'. The thinness and simplicity of his orchestration, designed to enhance the exotic atmosphere of Japan, can lead a listener to underrate the music, but those listening carefully will appreciate the quality of his craftsmanship.

There is a world of difference between the music of *Madama Butterfly* and a typical Italian opera such as Donizetti's *Lucia di Lammermoor*, which is set in Scotland, but in which little is Scottish except the costumes.

The Chicago resident completely failed to appreciate these aspects when he damned *Madama Butterfly* as 'dreadful'.

In the US with Gatti-Casazza (who ran La Scala and the Met),
Belasco (playwright), and Toscanini (the conductor)

WHO'S WHO AND WHAT'S WHAT

This summary is based on the libretto. As mentioned in the Warning at the end of this book, certain directors may amend opera stories to suit their production.

At a residence high above the harbour of Nagasaki,[4] **Goro**, a marriage broker and pimp, arranges a sham 'Japanese' wedding between the fifteen-year-old **Cio-Cio-San** (known as **Madame Butterfly**) and **Lieutenant Benjamin Franklin Pinkerton** of the US gunboat *Abraham Lincoln*.

Sharpless, the US Consul, can see that, in this case, the outcome will be disastrous.

The 'marriage' is conducted by the **Imperial Commissioner** and the **Registrar**. It is attended by various relatives of Butterfly. Her uncle, **the Bonzo** (a Buddhist monk), breaks up the ceremony and curses Butterfly because she has visited the Mission and converted to Pinkerton's religion. As a result, her people treat her as an outcast.

Meanwhile, to the glorious love duet *Ah! Dolce notte!* ('Oh Night of rapture, hasten to enfold us'), the happy couple retires to consummate the 'marriage'.

After Pinkerton returns to his ship, deserting her, Butterfly subsists alone with her servant **Suzuki**, and gives birth to a baby boy. It seems that Sharpless is providing limited finance, although he is unaware of the child.

Three years pass by. Goro tries to persuade Butterfly to marry the rich **Prince Yamadori** but, despite Suzuki's pessimism, she, now proud to be an American, is confident that her 'husband' will reappear one fine day: *Un bel dì*. He does eventually; but with his American wife **Kate**, who says she will take the child and look after it properly.

Butterfly agrees that Pinkerton can have the boy if he returns in half an hour. By then, she has stabbed herself with a dagger that was given to her father, on which is inscribed, 'Death with honour is better than life with dishonour.' Before doing this, in an emotional farewell, she gives the boy the US flag and a doll.

---

4 Nagasaki, a natural harbour surrounded by hills of about 1,500ft, is well positioned as a seaport on the south-western coast of Japan. Having been virtually closed to foreigners for centuries, the port was opened in 1859 and grew enormously in the subsequent years. It was the subject of an atomic bomb attack on 9 August, 1945.

Talking Points

Giacomo Puccini (1858–1924)
Please see the summary of the life of Puccini on pages 159 and 160.

Puccini's Place as a Composer – a View
The view expressed on pages 161-163 is very relevant.

The first night fiasco
Puccini, who was still hobbling around as a consequence of his very serious motor crash, was supremely confident in the success of his opera, so much so that he uncharacteristically invited his close relatives along to witness the first night. However, *Madama Butterfly* was received with a crescendo of abuse which led, at the end of the evening, to complete uproar and chaos.

It seems probable that the disruption was organised by Puccini's opponents, using the 'claque' who were paid to applaud or hiss. Their boss was highly remunerated by actors and management, but Puccini habitually refused to participate in this racket.

After act 1, there were hisses and catcalls. In the second act, Butterfly's kimono billowed up, and there was a shout of 'Butterfly is pregnant', a comment on Puccini's personal reputation.

Particular venom was reserved for an orchestral intermezzo at the end of Butterfly's vigil. This is omitted in the version we hear today. The producer Tito Ricordi had accompanied it with stage scenery which included birds twittering as dawn came up. The audience started imitating the twittering and eventually La Scala became more like a menagerie than an opera house. The end of the opera was greeted with hoots and howls. 'The opera is dead,' wrote one journalist.

Puccini cancelled the second night, withdrew the opera and returned his fee.

He made various changes, including slimming down act 1. His earlier decision to compress the opera into two acts, the second lasting an hour and a half, had caused friction between him and his librettist Giacosa, who had regarded it as 'interminable, monotonous and boring', and had warned him of the consequences.

It was indeed far too long for the attention span of a La Scala audience:

57

Verdi had appreciated the impatience of Italian audiences, and was concerned that the first act of his *Otello* lasted for forty-two minutes, as he said, 'two minutes more than is necessary.'

Dramatic irony
On the surface, the story is a very ordinary tale about typical behaviour in a seaport. The drama, however, is created by the use of a technique familiar to the ancient Greeks, known as 'dramatic irony'. From the outset, the audience is 'in the secret of what is inevitable', first, that Pinkerton will desert Madame Butterfly, and then that he has deserted her. This should be apparent to her, but she does not understand, and does not want to understand. Apart from its melody,[5] the effectiveness of *Un bel dì* is attributable to this dramatic irony.

Later, Puccini underlines the irony by providing the beautiful Humming Chorus (at the end of act 2 part 1), as an interlude to enable the audience to be able to sit and contemplate, unencumbered by words, the inevitable drama which is about to unfold, and compare the vulnerability of one protagonist and the heartlessness and insensitivity of the other.

The dominant role of Butterfly
Butterfly develops from being merely just one member of her chattering family to being the truly tragic woman at the end of the opera. Puccini put 'his whole resources into a musico-dramatic analysis of her shifting emotions and thoughts' (careful listening to the orchestra enables one to appreciate this). Thus, the story moves from an apparently perfunctory beginning to an overwhelming end. And the final chord[6] of the tragedy, provided the listener hears it through the applause, is in itself suitably disconcerting to match the tragic circumstances.

Once Butterfly appears, she is on stage for much of the opera, although she is allowed a brief rest in the early morning of the 'last day'. It is a colossal part, tougher than Tosca, and one which even a singer comfortable in a role such as that of Isolde has called 'one of the leading voice-killers'.

By comparison with her, all the other characters are perhaps peripheral. Indeed, it has been suggested that all that can be expected of Pinkerton is that 'he be a tenor, and sing the beautiful music allotted to him in the first

---

5 The listener can hear how the melody moves by very simple intervals, generally a feature of good tunes. Only one melodic leap is complex, a seventh when Butterfly says that, when Pinkerton sails in, she will not go down to the harbour to meet him, but will proudly await him in the house.

6 The work ends in B minor. But the final chord is a chord of G major in its first inversion, with a cataclysmic effect.

act with tender and passionate expression'. Sharpless the Consul has no great aria to sing. But as a fundamentally decent chap, and increasingly compassionate as the story develops, he has an enormous contribution to make in underpinning the emotional impact.

Placido Domingo has sung the role of Pinkerton in a 1974 film version of the opera conducted by Herbert von Karajan and directed by Jean-Pierre Ponnelle. But the stars generally avoid the male parts even if they may have filled them in their earlier years. They know that they will be eclipsed by the prima donna.

The clash of Eastern and Western cultures

Looked at today, the treatment in *Madama Butterfly* of the Japanese and the Americans can be considered, in their own different ways, to be in poor taste. Particularly in the wedding scene, the Japanese people are depicted in an unflattering light. And American people, personified in the arrogant, callous and 'colonial' Lieutenant Pinkerton, who is introduced with the United States national anthem 'The Star-spangled Banner', fare little better, albeit in a different way.[7]

It is surely almost blasphemous for Pinkerton's first names to be 'Benjamin Franklin', those of one of the Founding Fathers of the United States, and his ship to be the *Abraham Lincoln*. It is no coincidence that this name symbolising American freedom is shrieked out by Butterfly at the pivotal moment of the opera, when, utterly destroyed by the news that she has been deserted, she suddenly sees through her telescope an image that she interprets as Pinkerton returning to her. Puccini again uses the moment to play a snippet of 'The Star-spangled Banner'.

The music critic Gustav Kobbé, who was born and died in New York, went so far as to write that the use of 'The Star-spangled Banner' was 'highly objectionable and might, in time, become offensive, although no offence was meant.' However, a Bucharest production in 1957 used Pinkerton as a propaganda figure against imperialism. This is perhaps not surprising given that in the original version of the love duet, Butterfly tells Pinkerton that her immediate reaction when Goro suggested him as a candidate for marriage was to regard him as a brute – *un Americano, un barbaro*.

Pinkerton was far more arrogant in the Belasco play and in the original version of the opera. Puccini and his librettists actually toned down both the anti-Japanese and anti-American aspects, especially in their revised

---

7 At the end, Pinkerton is given a brief arioso, *Addio fiorito asil*, expressing farewell to his flowery bower, for a trysting place is all that, for him, it ever was. He expresses remorse. But this does not do much to dilute the heartless, cowardly impression he leaves.

version. From act 1, they cut various rude remarks about Japanese food ('candied frogs and flies') and greed. Pinkerton's wife Kate had a more prominent role and was characterised as being more aggressive and heartless about taking the baby.

Some of the cuts can be regretted because they weaken the clash of cultures which Puccini was depicting. In retrospect, however, they were probably politically wise, not least when viewed from the twenty-first century.

Very different attitudes

The magazine story which was the basis of *Madama Butterfly* has been traced back beyond the article in the 1898 magazine to *Madame Chrysanthème* (1887) a romance by the French writer Pierre Loti. He was the author of very popular novels towards the end of the nineteenth century, a time when imperialism and colonialism were the height of fashion, and attitudes were so very different and unacceptable from ours today.

Loti's many novels followed a standard formula: in a colourful foreign country, a western man and a native woman 'marry' according to local custom, their relationship being temporary. In Loti's, *Le Mariage de Loti*, published in 1880, a British naval officer has a love affair, arranged by the local Queen, with a fifteen year-old native girl in Tahiti. But the naval officer must sail away with his ship. That story inspired Delibes's opera *Lakmé* (1883), well-known today for its tune, 'the bell song'. That story was set in India where an English army officer falls, at first sight, for the daughter of a Hindu priest. When she appreciates that the regiment will leave, and their romance is but a tryst, she bites a poisonous plant and dies.

In real life, such relationships were not entirely fictional: Paul Gauguin, the post-impressionist painter, similarly took a 'wife' in Tahiti. So Lieutenant B. F. Pinkerton's behaviour was not entirely exceptional.

ACT BY ACT

The short prelude is based on a 'Japanese' theme which runs through act 1.

Act 1 Above Nagasaki harbour
The time is the present, that is, contemporary with the composition of the opera: the beginning of the twentieth century.

Goro, an obsequious marriage broker and pimp shows Lieutenant Benjamin Franklin Pinkerton, from the US Navy gunboat *Abraham Lincoln*, round a house high above the harbour of Nagasaki. Goro introduces him to the servants, led by Suzuki. Pinkerton is not too interested. The house is for Pinkerton to occupy with his bride, Cio-Cio-San. Their marriage ceremony is about to take place.

The US Consul, Sharpless, arrives, somewhat breathless from climbing up the hill to the house. With an irreverent introduction, using the start of the tune of 'The Star-spangled Banner', Sharpless and Pinkerton sit down for a drink: 'Milk-punch or whisky?'

Pinkerton jovially describes how he has bought the house for 999 years, with a monthly option to cancel the lease, rather like his marriage contract. Sharpless is disturbed to hear Pinkerton boast how he enjoys casual sex as he travels the world. His prospective 'wife', has only cost him one hundred yen.

Pinkerton is intoxicated with her: she is like a butterfly. He felt an urge to rush after her and catch her, even though it might damage her wings. Sharpless has overheard her visiting his consulate and is concerned that she will get hurt. Pinkerton drinks to a proper marriage with an American girl sometime in the future.

Butterfly arrives with her girlfriends. Her outpouring of joy soars over the 'bridesmaids', to D flat if she can get there (Puccini provides a lower alternative).

She introduces them to Pinkerton. She tells how she is aged fifteen and has only a mother, her father being dead. Her relations appear, as do the Imperial Commissioner and the Registrar. One of Butterfly's uncles[8] is in search of a drink. Pinkerton finds it all delightful and hilarious.

---

8 In the original version performed at the première, this uncle's part was far larger, which increased the comedy but slowed up the action. The scene also involved a naughty little boy, who Puccini cut out in the revised version.

There is much chatter between Butterfly's relatives, some of it cleverly set by Puccini in the form of a canon, with the singers imitating each other, note for note, a bar or so apart, so that the words they use appear jumbled and unintelligible. Some relatives claim that they themselves were also offered to Pinkerton by Goro; they express varying opinions of Pinkerton and of Butterfly. Sharpless continues to be disconcerted by it all.

Butterfly shows Pinkerton her few possessions. She withholds one, a sheath with a knife, which Goro explains that the Mikado (or Emperor) sent to her father with a message telling him to use it. Butterfly assures Pinkerton that she has been secretly to the Mission and has converted to his religion. She throws away the images of her ancestors.

With the Commissioner announcing Pinkerton of the *Lincoln*, to the horns playing an excerpt from 'The Star-spangled Banner', the marriage formalities take place. Afterwards, Sharpless, the Commissioner and the Registrar leave. Before going, Sharpless warns Pinkerton to be careful.

When the party is about to resume, Butterfly's uncle the Bonzo (a Buddhist monk) is heard. He is furious because Butterfly has renounced her religion. He curses her, whereupon her relatives immediately desert her. Cast out by her own people, she collapses in tears, and is comforted by Pinkerton, who, being just interested in the coming night, does not take her concerns too seriously: *Viene la sera*.

Suzuki, her servant, prepares Butterfly for the night. Apprehensive that she may die of her love, she just wants to be loved: *Vogliatemi bene*. Pinkerton is ecstatic, but Butterfly cannot get the sound of her relatives out of her ears. When he calls her 'Butterfly', she has a premonition: she has heard that in his country, he who catches a butterfly will pierce its heart with a needle and leave it to die. True, Pinkerton says, but that is so that she cannot run away. He has got her! He catches her in his arms and they complete the glorious love duet *Ah! Dolce notte!* in which they invoke the sweet night to enfold them in ecstasy. It does, as she reaches top C. In what has been described as the finest duet Puccini ever composed, they enter the house for the night, beneath the infinite, starry sky. For her, the stars laugh with endless joy.

Act 2 Part 1 Three years later
Butterfly is still in her house. Suzuki prays to her Japanese gods: *E Izaghi ed Izanami*. Their money is running out.

Suzuki is doubtful that Pinkerton will return, but Butterfly angrily reproaches her for her negative attitude: otherwise, why did he order the Consul to provide the house for them, and have it fitted with locks so that her frightful relatives could be kept out? Pinkerton said that he will return with the roses, and when the robins nest. One fine day, they will see a wisp of smoke and a ship on the sea: *Un bel dì, vedremo levarsi un fil di fumo.*[9] His ship will glide into the harbour. She will wait for him up in the house. They will see him in the distance, and hear him calling, 'Butterfly'. She will pretend to hide, and then he will embrace her with all the loving words he once used.

Goro arrives with Sharpless. Butterfly welcomes him, and is overcome with excitement at the sight of a letter that Sharpless has had from Pinkerton. She asks what time of year the robins nest in the United States – maybe in that country they nest less frequently than in Japan? Sharpless says that he does not understand ornithology.

Goro tells how he has been trying to persuade Butterfly to marry another man, the wealthy Prince Yamadori, who arrives, to a fanfare, to woo her. She dismisses the suggestion that she is divorced, and stands by the law of 'her country', the USA. Again we hear the strains of 'The Star-spangled Banner'. To Sharpless's desperation, Butterfly displays her optimism about her rights under US divorce law.

Pinkerton's ship has already signalled its arrival. But Butterfly delays Sharpless from telling her the bad news that Pinkerton does not want to see her. He begins to read the letter from Pinkerton; Butterfly interrupts him. Eventually, Sharpless asks her what she would do if Pinkerton were never to return. To her, this notion is like a deathblow. She responds that she would either return to her former life, or die. Sharpless urges her to marry Prince Yamadori.

They will surely not forget, she says, her baby, whom she now brings to show Sharpless (he has been unaware, until now, of its existence, as has Pinkerton). She shows him how the child has Pinkerton's features. She asks Sharpless to write and tell Pinkerton about the child.

She sings to the baby how the heartless Sharpless has implied that she should return to earn her living by taking the child into the town and by dancing and becoming a geisha again: *Che tua madre*. She would ten times prefer death – *Morta, Morta* – to that. Sharpless asks the baby's name:

---

9 There is a story about how Puccini heard *Un bel dì* being played far too slowly on a barrel organ outside his hotel window. He rushed out though the amazed guests and staff, admonished the organ grinder, grabbed the handle of the barrel organ and turned it like fury to get it up to speed. The next day, the organ grinder was there again, with displayed on his machine: 'Pupil of Puccini'.

it is now Trouble, but when Pinkerton returns it will be Joy. Sharpless is overcome with emotion[10] and leaves, saying that he will inform Pinkerton.

In a complete contrast of mood, Suzuki rages at Goro, who has insinuated that, in the United States, a bastard child is treated as an outcast. Butterfly seizes the dagger and goes for Goro, who is lucky to escape. The cannon is fired, signalling the arrival of a ship in the harbour. She looks through her telescope and to her utter joy she can read the name *Abraham Lincoln*.

Butterfly is confident that the others were liars, her faith is to be rewarded, and Pinkerton is about to return to her. In the obverse of a 'mad scene', she and Suzuki scatter cherry blossom[11] all over the place, singing the 'flower song', *Scuoti quella fronda di ciliegio*. Suzuki helps Butterfly to dress in her wedding dress. They make little spy holes to see Pinkerton when he comes.

While night falls, an offstage chorus sings the Humming Chorus. The baby and Suzuki sleep, but Butterfly watches and waits, as does the audience, for whom this beautiful chorus provides a moment to contemplate the terrible dénouement about to unfold.

Act 2 Part 2 Immediately afterwards
After the searingly sad interlude, sailors are heard in the very far distance. Their remoteness, and the paucity of the orchestration, emphasise the hopelessness of the situation.

There are sounds on the horns and bells as the world awakens: whistles depict birds beginning to sing. Suzuki urges Butterfly, who has been waiting up all night, to go and rest. She lulls her darling child to sleep, *Dormi, amor mio* reaching top B as she goes out through the door. Suzuki surely reflects the mood of the audience, a sense of profound, almost uncontrollable, sadness for Butterfly, as she despairs: *Povera Butterfly*.

Sharpless and Pinkerton creep in, telling Suzuki, 'ssh'. She tells them how Butterfly has watched every ship entering the harbour for the past three years, and how they scattered and arranged the flowers last night. She sees that they are accompanied by a woman and is horrified: it is Pinkerton's American wife.

---

10 Sir Thomas Allen has described how this scene provides the potential for 'one of the most moving half-hours in opera'. Unchecked, the performer's own emotional involvement, particularly at the moment when the baby is shown to Sharpless, could even have a detrimental effect on the performance: 'The lump in the throat is in danger of strangling one,' he wrote.
11 To provide the petals at a performance in Bristol, a box full of torn-up paper was shaken at the end of a long bamboo pole. The string broke, with the result that the box hit Butterfly on the head. She had to shuffle her way through paper, cardboard and string.

Sharpless explains that they must secure the welfare of the child and asks for Suzuki's help. She must fetch Butterfly. Pinkerton, a contemptibly feeble character, can only look uselessly around at the strewn flowers and his photograph.[12] Sharpless reminds Pinkerton that he warned him to be careful.

Pinkerton eventually, remorsefully, goes away, leaving some money behind. Kate Pinkerton asks Suzuki to explain the situation to Butterfly and tell her that she will take the child and look after it properly.

Butterfly appears before this can be done. She cannot be stopped from coming in. She is surprised to see Sharpless with Kate. She comforts Suzuki, who weeps uncontrollably. She checks that Pinkerton is alive. The truth dawns.

Kate admits that she is the cause of the trouble. She asks for the son. Butterfly congratulates her and agrees that Pinkerton can have him if he returns in half an hour. When the others go, Butterfly collapses. She recovers and orders Suzuki away to play with the child.

She goes to fetch the dagger which the Mikado sent her father, on which are inscribed the words, 'Death with honour is better than life with dishonour.' She is about to stab herself when the child comes in. She sings an anguished farewell to her darling child, her little god, *Tu tu piccolo Iddio*, 'possibly the most heart-rending music of Puccini's entire oeuvre', according to one of Puccini's leading biographers. She gives him a United States flag and a doll and urges him to play with them. She blindfolds him.

She takes the knife, goes behind the screen and stabs herself. She emerges, totters towards the child and embraces him: *Amore addio! addio! piccolo amor! Va, gioca, gioca!* ('Go and play'). The music in the orchestra, before the thump, tells us that her last thoughts are with '*tu piccolo Iddio*', with her little god, with her child.

The feeble Pinkerton is heard without. He appears with Sharpless just in time for Butterfly to gesture to the child, collapse and die. It is Sharpless who, sobbing, takes the child. The orchestra concludes the opera in unison with the theme heard earlier accompanying the word *morta* in Butterfly's great aria *Che tua madre*. And the orchestra ends the opera on a truly cataclysmic note. The structure of the final chord (G major in its first inversion) is surely without precedent as a closure to an opera.

---

12 At least Puccini gives him a couple of top B flats!

Perhaps a deterioration around the middle of his career
is attributable to Puccini's partiality for women and cars

La Fanciulla del West

Puccini in Vienna with Jeritza,
the greatly admired Tosca, Minnie and Turandot

Contents

La Fanciulla del West,
THE GIRL OF THE GOLDEN WEST :

Background

A 'good girl', who is devoted to self-improvement, the hardworking and the downtrodden, reforms a 'bad guy', a bandit, a thief who robs the community. Love is the catalyst which redeems the sinner! Love even intervenes dramatically just as the criminal is about to swing.

Puccini had written several operas about frail and beautiful women: Mimì, Butterfly and even Manon. Although Tosca was of tougher fibre, Puccini still felt the need to compose an opera about the more robust female. The result was Minnie, a strapping, fine-looking country girl, a beacon of hope in the violent, seedy atmosphere of the American Gold Rush around 1850.

Seven years had elapsed since *Madama Butterfly*. Meanwhile, the productions of his existing works had kept him busy. During this time, he cast around unsuccessfully for a suitable libretto for his next opera. As always, he took immense care. More than most composers, he knew how crucial it is to get that choice right: to a great extent, his success was due to his commercial intuition and acumen.

He toyed with various suggestions including a comedy, and even a grand opera about Marie Antoinette, but he could not find anything which he liked and was suitable. Then he was invited by The Metropolitan Opera to attend a festival of his operas in New York early in 1907. This was ideal, because he wanted to break directly into the American market. On stage nearby, were various plays written by David Belasco, the dramatist whose work Puccini had used as the basis for *Butterfly*. One of these was 'The Girl of the Golden West'.

David Belasco (1853–1931) was born in San Francisco of Portuguese-Jewish origin. He was educated by monks in British Columbia. He was the ultimate show-man. He was a clown; after that, an actor touring the Californian towns where memories of the Gold Rush were recent. He became a writer, director, producer, and a powerful impresario. He thrived on atmospheric and emotional plots worthy of Hollywood. In later life, footmen would usher his visitors theatrically into his inner sanctum, where dressed in clerical attire redolent of Liszt, he would receive them from behind a huge desk. He thought his outfit was consistent with being an alumnus of a monastery.

Belasco was expert at producing a sensational show. Before the curtain went up, the theatre audience was presented with a cinematic panorama of the Californian Cloudy Mountains, and was entertained by a minstrel band. The blizzard was created by thirty-two operatives working wind and snow machines.

Puccini was attracted to successful stage dramas like this. The story had some similarity to *Tosca*: there was an evil male; and a woman's honour and her lover's life were at stake. Tosca, of course, was experienced. But, in this case, Minnie was a virgin. There was sex – not explicit, of course – and even a happy outcome. A pretentious 'redemption through love' theme had been used successfully by Wagner, despite not having the benefit of Belasco's stark realism and sentimentality. What better? The ingredients seemed good; Puccini gave it some thought.

Puccini had begun a passionate affair with an English society hostess, Sybil Seligman, whom he had encountered when attending *Butterfly* performances in London. She nudged him into selecting 'The Girl of the Golden West'. She commissioned the Italian translation, and suggested the title 'La Fanciulla del West'. She also helped him find American mid-century music and Native American songs with which to provide appropriate local colour.

The death of Giuseppe Giacosa deprived him of his usual pair of librettists. So the Italian text was prepared by Carlo Zangarini, an experienced librettist, whose mother was from New York and who also knew English. Another writer, Guelfo Civinini, was brought in to help with the process and to tone the libretto down in places. Puccini himself suggested changes, particularly in the last act, so that the play was suitable for an operatic stage: he wanted the man-hunt, Minnie riding to the rescue, and her farewell. By end January 1908, he had a libretto on which he could start work.

However, between October of that year and the following July, he was completely distracted by a domestic crisis.

Four years earlier, Puccini had finally married his long-term mistress, Elvira. This did not affect his tendency to womanise. She began to suspect that he was having an affair with one of the domestic maids. Her virtually insane desire for revenge led to the suicide of the maid and her own prosecution. Puccini was only in the right frame of mind to resume work once that ghastly episode was out of the way. He was very pleased with the result. With Sybil's help, Alexandra, Queen of England, a *La Bohème* enthusiast, accepted the dedication of the new opera and gave him a diamond and ruby pin in recognition.

La Fanciulla del West, produced by Belasco himself, was premièred at The Metropolitan Opera House, New York, on 10 December, 1910. Toscanini conducted. Three high-profile celebrities starred. The Czech diva and leading Butterfly, Emmy Destinn, was the heroine Minnie. Enrico Caruso was the bandit, Johnson. And Pasquale Amato, a Met stalwart, was the sheriff, Jack Rance. Eight horses appeared on the stage in act 3.

The marketing had been sensational. This was the first time the Met had staged the première of a world famous composer. Posters were to be seen depicting the heroine and the sheriff playing poker for the life of her lover. He had collapsed on the table, bleeding from a gunshot wound.

Sex Poker. The stakes: her body, Johnson's life

Tickets sold at thirty times the box office price which anyway had been doubled for the special event. For the second night, the box office price was quadrupled.

The production was a great success, 'one of the most spectacular events' in the annals of the Met. There were fourteen curtain calls at the end of act 1, nineteen after act 2, after which Puccini was crowned with a silver crown covered with ribbons in the national colours of Italy and the United States. There were fifty-two curtain calls in all. The production went on to Boston and Chicago.

Meanwhile, Elvira Puccini was left at home, deeply disappointed that he had not asked her to be present on this great occasion.

The opera has not endured as an example of Puccini's outstanding success. Most people associate him with *La Bohème, Tosca, Madama Butterfly, Turandot*, but not particularly with *La Fanciulla*. Most notably, it lacked 'the incandescent lyrical phrase'. The critics recognised the difficulties of making an opera out of a story such as this one, and were initially less enthusiastic.

There was far too much detail and activity: Kiri Te Kanawa's complaint about Puccini's 'bloody words, bloody, bloody words' is apposite. Successful opera plots, to a great extent, are relatively simple, however absurd they may be.

The secret of success, as exemplified by Mozart, was to use recitative to take the action forward and to use arias to communicate the singer's feelings about events or people, or (say) love. In *La Fanciulla*, music which is the equivalent of recitative is used to create the atmosphere – for example in the long half-hour in act 1, before Johnson arrives. A good production will allow for this, and even overcome it, but success relies greatly on the ability of the producer, and the budget.[1]

So, after the initial excitement, a production of *La Fanciulla* became a relatively rare event for the following sixty years, although the last act was found to work particularly well, for example, in the open air at Verona. Recently, it has done better: indeed, Placido Domingo has asserted that 'although it not among Puccini's most popular operas, it has been a huge success'.

It is hard to surpass the drama. Possibly it is overdramatic: a robbery, an attempted rape, a love scene, a chase, a hanging... Few will leave the performance without being deeply moved. It may be a moot point whether it is the story, or the music, or both, that really moves them.

---

1 The need to have a realistic production curtails the potential for the designer and producer to abstract themselves away from the type of realistic set which Puccini envisaged and which audiences, if not many producers, tend to prefer. The 'Polka' saloon and Minnie's cabin limit the scope for Puccini's desire for realism to be ignored.

WHO'S WHO AND WHAT'S WHAT

This summary is based on the libretto. As mentioned in the Warning at the end of this book, certain directors may amend opera stories to suit their production.

The opera starts with a detailed and colourful picture of saloon life in the wild-west during the Gold Rush in mid-nineteenth century. The 'Polka' saloon is in a prospectors' camp at the foot of the Cloudy Mountains in California. On the wall, there is a 'Wanted' notice: **Wells-Fargo**, the mail company who transports the gold-diggers' metal, will pay a reward for the capture of **Ramerrez**, a Mexican bandit.

Jack Rance,[2] the sheriff, sits brooding. **Nick**, the bar tender, takes orders for drinks. Gold-diggers play cards. **Billy Jackrabbit**, a Red Indian (Native American), filches drink and cigars.

The diggers are homesick. **Jake Wallace**, a wandering ballad-singer, sings a lament to the Californian folk tune **'The Old Dog "Tray"'**, which recurs later in the opera. Is his old mother back home worrying, and wondering if he will return? If he does, will his old dog 'Tray' recognise him?

This nostalgia is too much for **Larkens** from Cornwall, England, who breaks down. **Sonora** arranges a whip-round, a collection, to send him home. The arrival of the post also makes the men feel homesick. **Sid**, a card-sharper, is caught cheating and narrowly avoids being strung up.

The brutality of the gold-diggers and their environment is contrasted with **Minnie**, the owner/manager of the 'Polka' saloon, one of the few women in town. She has a heart of gold and is the only person they can trust to look after their metal which is placed in a keg by the bar. She teaches them the Bible and about forgiveness: no sinner is beyond redemption. She does not reciprocate Rance's intention to marry her: indeed, she repels his advances with her revolver.

***

Ramerrez is known to be in the area. **Ashby**, the Wells Fargo manager, is on his trail. A stranger enters, claiming to be **Dick Johnson** from Sacramento. (In fact, he is Ramerrez 'casing the joint' before leading a raid on the saloon.) Minnie and Johnson have met before, on the road, and were instantly attracted to each other. Minnie now vouches for Johnson and dances with him. Rance is most unhappy.

---

2 The names, including Rance, have English pronunciation. Rance rhymes with 'pants' not 'dance'.

Jose Castro, a member of the Ramerrez gang, acts as a decoy to get the diggers to clear the saloon. Johnson alone remains behind with Minnie, with the keg of gold. They are interrupted by Nick who warns that bandits are around. Indeed a whistle is heard signifying that a raid is about to begin. She captivates Johnson, and he declares that nobody will dare steal the gold. When he has to go, she invites him to her log cabin halfway up the mountain.

In Minnie's cabin, an hour later, local colour is again provided, this time by her Native servant **Wowkle,** her papoose and Billy, the child's father. There is a **blizzard** outside. Minnie dresses up to receive Johnson, and she has to resist his ardour. He is edgy, but, because of the weather, he cannot leave. She has to hide him when various gold-diggers come to warn her that Ramerrez been seen nearby.

Johnson admits to her that he is Ramerrez. For her, his unfortunate upbringing is no excuse, so she dismisses him out into the night. A shot is heard. She pulls him in and pushes him up into the loft. Rance comes into the cabin. He tries to kiss (even rape) her. A drop of blood dripping from the ceiling indicates that the wounded fugitive is hiding above.[3] Johnson faints as he comes down. He slumps onto a chair at the table.

Minnie and Rance **play poker** for Johnson's life. She cheats and wins, and claims Johnson.

Rance keeps his word and does not disclose the criminal's whereabouts. About a week later, Johnson has made a run for it and is being chased. He is caught and is summarily condemned to be hanged. But Nick secretly bribes the hangman, Billy, to delay.

Just as Johnson is about to die, Minnie gallops up, pistol between her teeth, followed by Nick. She claims that she has given her best years for the gold-diggers; in return, they should give her Johnson, who is now a reformed character. He was going off to lead a new life. The gold-diggers cave in. Rance is demented with rage.

With Johnson, Minnie bids farewell to her tearful gold-diggers. The lovers ride off together into the distance.[4]

---

3 Belasco's father had been involved in the Gold Rush. Both the blood dripping from the ceiling, and the subsequent poker game, are apparently based on real incidents which Belasco's father had experienced. Jake Wallace, the minstrel with the banjo, is also based on a real life character from the period.

4 Lesser parts, apart from the squaw Wowkle, are exclusively masculine (including the chorus). There are Wells-Fargo men and several gold-diggers, including specifically: Bello, Joe, Trin, Harry, Handsome, and Happy.

Talking Points

Giacomo Puccini (1858–1924)
Please see the summary of the life of Puccini on pages 159 and 160.

Puccini's Place as a Composer – a View
The view expressed on pages 161-163 is very relevant.

The Gold Rush
In 1830, there were around five hundred foreigners on the west side of the Sierra Nevada. During the 1840s, the importance of California became clear to the authorities in Washington and, following military action, it was annexed and declared part of the United States in 1846. Mexico agreed to cede New Mexico and California to the US in early 1848. There was then a dispute whether slavery should be allowed in California. A bill passed Congress in 1850 admitting it into the Union as a free state (that is, one in which slavery was prohibited or being phased out).

In January 1848, a few flakes of gold were found on John A. Sutter's ranch in a place now called Coloma, east of Sacramento. The frenzy began: 'men raced by land and sea to wash millions out of the gulches and dig more from the hills'. By May in the following year, there were more than 5,000 wagons on the California trail. By the end of 1850, there were 50,000 men extracting gold, largely from the river beds. The Californian population grew from 12,000 to 92,000 by late 1850, and 380,000 by 1860. The Pacific Mail Steamship Company, formed in 1848, carried $122 million worth of gold dust in its first four years. The environment was lawless.

The 1849-50 date given in the score of *La Fanciulla* precedes the formation of Mr Ashby's Wells, Fargo & Company, which was only founded in 1852 (to provide express and banking services to California). It was formed by the New York merchants Henry Wells and William G. Fargo, the two founders of American Express. But that is detail: for the opera, colour and an evocative name like Wells Fargo are more important than accuracy.

The Affaire Doria
Soon after Puccini began composing *La Fanciulla*, his attention was diverted by a tragic incident involving him and Doria Manfredi, a servant at his house in Torre del Lago, near Lucca.

Puccini had a mistress, Elvira, who he married in 1904, after the death of her first husband permitted her remarriage. She had been around for twenty years, and he was bored with her: she had not kept pace with his success, and he was anyway a considerable womaniser. She was desperately jealous. When she found him late at night talking to one of the domestic servants, the twenty-one year-old Doria Manfredi, Elvira became hysterical and started following Doria around the village, shrieking abuse. Doria was driven to committing an agonising suicide by drinking poison.

After this, the Manfredi family prosecuted Elvira, who was convicted, fined and sentenced to several months imprisonment. The case was settled, so she did not have to go to jail, but not surprisingly the whole matter caused Puccini enormous worry. It may well have resulted in the 'signs of exhaustion in his inventive faculty and a reduction in his powers of concentration' which a leading biographer has observed in *La Fanciulla*.

The Music
The relative lack of popularity of the music of *La Fanciulla* arises from the absence of memorable arias: the few tunes that are played in the orchestra are brief and fizzle out. Commentators criticise the opera's 'flagging melodic invention', even if this is more than sufficiently compensated for by the intense drama and excitement of the story.

Minnie, whose music one might expect to be lyrical, has been expunged of sweetness. Perhaps Puccini deliberately wanted to distinguish her from his other heroines.

One might perhaps expect Rance's attempt to win her in act 1 to provide an opportunity for a melodic duet. But she is looking for real love, such as that given her by her parents, who are innkeepers 'down home in Soledad'; and she emphasises her point by hitting top C. Later, during the first part of the scene in the cabin, when Minnie and Johnson woo each other, some delightful melody begins to be heard in the orchestra. But it is not developed into a love song: Minnie takes her first kiss also on a top C.

Indeed, much of Minnie's music is high up the scale. As a consequence, the risk that the singer will sound stressed is correspondingly increased. Both Minnie and Johnson are expected to hang onto their high notes in a way which at times almost becomes a mannerism.

Some of the recurring musical themes are based on Californian folk tunes of the time, for example 'The Old Dog "Tray"'. This tune re-appears frequently, notably at the beginning, when the miners feel homesick, and at the end when Minnie and Johnson leave California.

In general, commentators regarded the music of *La Fanciulla* as 'modern'. The atmosphere is set by the harsh opening bars of act 1; the act ends on a discord.

Puccini makes considerable use of the whole-tone scale, consisting of the six notes within the octave, each a whole tone apart. The augmented fourth, which for much of classical music had been associated with evil (and, in *Tosca,* with Scarpia the chief of police), is a component of the whole-tone scale. It features prominently in creating the character of Rance and the atmosphere at the start of act 3.[5]

However, the whole-tone scale, which is much heard in the music of Debussy, gives a feeling of tonal vagueness. The vigorous action in *La Fanciulla* was thought incompatible with such an impressionistic style. The orchestration was considered suggestive of Richard Strauss whose *Salome* had been premièred almost exactly five years earlier. Puccini reassured a friend that his discordant sounds, when played by an orchestra rather than by a piano, were much softer and smoother.

The Characters

Minnie has been called the 'oddest of all Puccini's heroines'. She is 'histrionically effective but psychologically impossible': on the one hand, she 'consorts with the riff-raff of a gold-mining-camp' and is 'a kind of 'gangster's moll, a Fury and Valkyrie of the Wild West rolled into one'; on the other, she is a pure angel, who, though uneducated, holds forth on moral redemption through love. Yet, under pressure, she will not hesitate to cheat at cards.

Unfortunately, Puccini did not introduce his audience to Nina, who we are told is the proprietress of the 'Palms', the rival saloon to Minnie's 'Polka'. She, according to Rance, is Johnson's previous lover, and has betrayed him. She is a tart, a contrast to Minnie. Despite the intentions of playwright and composer to strive for total realism, we may imagine that Nina would be the more realistic character of the two.

The relationship between Rance, Johnson, and Minnie is compared with that of Scarpia, Cavaradossi (the fugitive) and Tosca (his lover).

Of the two male protagonists in *La Fanciulla*, Jack Rance is surely the most interesting. At the start of act 3, Ashby, the Wells Fargo employee, reveals: 'Ever since that night in the bar, I have not been able to place you, Sheriff'. Rance is no card-board villain who pushes his passion for Minnie almost to the extent of rape. He is a man of honour who keeps his word; he is the sheriff and has his duty to do. Yet he goes berserk with vengefulness when he is in a position to

5 The theme which accompanies Rance when he declares that hanging is too clean and quick a punishment for the gambling cheat Sid, uses the whole-tone scale; as does the sinister sound which we hear when the sheriff leads the posse off to find 'Ramerrez'.

destroy his rival. Johnson is a latter day Robin Hood. Rance regards him as no better than a *fantoccio*, a puppet, a word which a modern dictionary denotes for a 'car-crash test-dummy'. Johnson possesses an apparent social superiority. But this does not fit comfortably with his sheer banditry, however noble it may be.

Some small parts in *La Fanciulla* are etched with great subtlety. Nick, the bar tender discovers a cigar butt on the floor of the cabin and loyally keeps quiet about it; and he bribes the 'executioner' to delay stringing up Johnson so as to allow Minnie time to arrive.

The pacing of the last, dramatic scenes of the opera is masterly. Puccini's ability to sustain the tension is an indication of his craftsmanship.

American aspects
In the libretto, Billy Jackrabbit and Wowkle his squaw are described as Red Indians, 'Indiani'. The correct usage today is, of course, 'Native American'. Billy's tendency to shop-lift, and have a papoose (baby) outside wedlock – whatever that may mean in the context of their own culture – might perhaps represent a portrayal of the bad moral influence the gold-diggers had exerted on an otherwise unblemished ethnic group.

The libretto, with its greedy, gambling gold-diggers and a twisted sheriff, is hardly flattering to the United States, nor are the grunts (specified as a half growl, half nasal sound) which the Natives are supposed to emit at frequent intervals.

Puccini changed Belasco's play to portray Billy as the hangman of Johnson. For the première, it was decided to appoint one of the gold-diggers to fulfil this task, it not being considered suitable for New Yorkers to see a Native American perform this role.

ACT BY ACT

Act 1 The interior of the 'Polka', a saloon

The gold-diggers congregate in two saloons in town, the 'Polka' and the 'Palms'.[6] The scene opens in the 'Polka', which is owned and run by Minnie.

The homesick diggers drink, play cards and sing a folktune, 'Dooda, dooda, day'. Jack Rance, the sheriff, sits brooding; Nick, the bar tender, takes orders. There is a 'Wanted' notice on the wall showing that Wells Fargo are offering a $5,000 ransom for the capture of Ramerrez, a bandit.

Jake Wallace, a wandering ballad-singer, sings a sad, nostalgic lament which he accompanies on his banjo (a harp behind the scenes):[7] the old folks and his mother back home will be wondering whether they will ever see him again. Will the Old Dog "Tray" be around when he returns? They all join in as they think of home.

This is too much for Larkens, from Cornwall, who breaks down, and wants his mum. Sonora passes the hat round for a collection to send him home.

The card game resumes. Sid is caught cheating[8] and the others call for him to be strung him up. Jack Rance, the sheriff tells them that death is too swift and painless a punishment. He has a better one: he pins a two of spades onto Sid, a warning and sign of shame used in the Gold Rush, and tells him he will be hanged if he is seen without it. He then kicks him out. There is no mercy.

Ashby, the Wells Fargo manager, arrives and tells Rance that he has been following Ramerrez, the Mexican bandit, for three months without success. At last, he is now on his track.

The gold-diggers drink a toast to Minnie. Rance claims that she will soon be Mrs Rance, and comes to blows, almost murderous, with Sonora, who also fancies her. She appears, with the orchestra proclaiming her fortissimo with a theme which will be associated with her. She intervenes and separates the combatants. One of the gold-diggers gives her flowers; Sonora presents her with some lace and ribbons, blue as her eyes. He also deposits his gold with her, although Ashby of course reckons that Wells Fargo bank would be a safer place for that.

---

6 They address each other collectively in Italian with the word 'ragazzi', which recurs frequently and means, 'boys', 'lads', 'you guys' etc.

7 This American folk-song melody known as 'The Old Dog "Tray"' or 'Echoes from Home' is a recurring theme denoting homesickness and will be heard again in the closing bars of the opera.

8 Later in the opera, Minnie cheats unashamedly.

She gives them all a Bible lesson, teaching them about King David and his fifty-first psalm.[9] To her, this means that there is no sinner who cannot find redemption. She chastises Billie, the Native who has been drinking the heel-taps, and Wowkle, his squaw, for having a baby outside marriage.

Redemption

The emphasis on redemption tends to irritate many commentators on *La Fanciulla*. Minnie's 'redemption through love', salvation through the devotion of a pure woman, is 'the idealistic Wagnerian motive transferred to the brutal realism of a wild-west drama', wrote one. Contrition was not an obvious feature in Puccini's character, but nor was it in Wagner's.

The mail arrives and the post-boy mentions the bandit. When the gold-diggers open their post, they again suffer from homesickness. Joe's granny has died.

Ashby ask Minnie about Nina Micheltorena, the tarty proprietress of the other saloon, the 'Palms'. She has sent a note to Ashby betraying the whereabouts of Ramerrez.

A stranger has arrived outside who wants a drink. He must be a toff, a swell from San Francisco, because he has asked for whisky and water (a claim to refinement and social superiority: rough gold-diggers normally drink it neat).

Rance, accompanied by thick and foreboding orchestral sounds, propositions Minnie (a thousand dollars for a kiss). She draws her revolver on him. She ticks him off because he has a wife. He describes how he left home, unloved and loving no-one, only gold; and he will give a fortune to have her. But, Minnie is looking for true love, like that of her parents in the pub which they ran – her home, sweet home, in Soledad. Ah (emphasised with a top C), how her parents loved each other; that is the kind of love she seeks.

At this moment Johnson, from Sacramento, comes in. The orchestra picks up speed, reflecting her immediate emotions. She gets Nick to fetch Johnson's drink. Rance says that strangers are not allowed in the camp, and he tries to head him off – in the direction of Nina Micheltorena. He fails, and withdraws in a rage.

Minnie and Johnson have met before, on the road to Monterey,[10] when

---

9 'Purge me with hyssop and I shall be clean...Wash me , and I shall be whiter than snow... create in me a clean heart, and renew a right spirit within me....'

10 Soledad, Minnie's home, now a wine growing area, is twenty-five miles from Monterey, the port on the Pacific coast which was once the capital of California. It is just over a hundred miles south of San Francisco. It is a long way, 250 miles, from Coloma (to the east of Sacramento), where the Gold Rush began.

he gave her a posy of jasmine, and said he would never forget her. Rance, who suspects Johnson is on his way to the tart at the other joint, asks him his business. Minnie vouches for Johnson and, although she has never danced before, she waltzes with him, as the gold-diggers hum a tune. Rance is most unhappy.

Suddenly, Castro, a Hispanic who the gold-diggers have captured, is brought in. He agrees to show them where Ramerrez is hiding (but in fact he is acting as a decoy to lead them on a wild-goose-chase while the bandits rob the bar). He whispers to Johnson that, at the appropriate moment, he will give the signal.

The gold-diggers consign their gold to the safekeeping of Minnie. They go off on their horses to chase the bandit.

Johnson and Minnie talk while Nick, the bar tender, shuts up shop. Minnie and Johnson are alone, and a solo oboe repeating the waltz tune tells us exactly what is going through her mind. The duet opens with Johnson feeling rather perturbed: he has come to rob her; but now maybe only of a kiss.

She makes the running at first. She lives alone in her cabin half way up the mountain. She is but an insignificant woman, uneducated, longing to reach up to the stars, to his level. When he admits that he had felt her heartthrob when they danced together just now, we hear the waltz tune again. He too had felt a wonderful feeling of joy.

They are interrupted by Nick who reports that another bandit has been seen skulking around. The signal, a discreet sound of a whistle, is heard. She, looking to Johnson for protection, explains that the gold is kept in the keg by the bar. The gold-diggers take turns to guard it. But they have all gone off now, and she is responsible for it. Johnson is surprised that she would take such risks on behalf of others. She explains how the gold means so much to the diggers because they have worked so hard in dreadful conditions, even to death, to extract it. Often, they work in order to send the money back home to the wife and children.

But nobody will get the gold except over her dead body. Nobody will dare, he declares, utterly captivated.

He knows he must go now. But he wanted to say goodbye to her in her cabin on the mountain; she invites him to continue their conversation there, but he must not expect too much of her, uneducated and inadequate as she is: if only she had studied more, who knows what she might have been. Johnson tells her that the important thing is that she is good and pure. Besides, she has the face of an angel. When he has left, she is overcome with emotion: he said that she had the face of an angel! The act ends on an unresolved discord, almost posing the question 'but, wait and see what happens next?'!

Act 2 Minnie's cabin

The wind howls outside Minnie's log cabin, just an hour later. The windows are frozen up; there is a blizzard outside. A table is set for one.

Just as act 1 began with a folktune to give colour, act 2 starts with Wowkle, the squaw, singing a Native American folktune to her baby by the hearth.

Billy, her man, smokes his pipe and eyes the food which Wowkle tells him not to touch. Minnie has told them to get married. Billy refers to the 'dowry'. They continue to sing their folksongs together.

Minnie comes in and says she wants supper for two. She puts on her best clothes. The Natives are surprised, because this has never happened before.

When Johnson comes in, he tries to embrace her, but this is too fast for Minnie (although a chromatic run on the flutes indicates her flutter). With the waltz tune humming in her ears, she blushingly agrees that he may stay.

She wonders why he came to her bar in the first place: was he actually on the way to Micheltorena's? He ducks this question, and wonders why she likes living all alone. She sings, with a little galloping theme, about her gallops on her pony through the glorious mountains she loves so much; she tells of her teaching 'academy' for the gold-diggers, and her books. Eventually, she talks of love.[11]

While Wowkle is there, Minnie resists Johnson's advances. Wowkle cannot go home because of the snow (as the wind machine indicates clearly), so Minnie tells her to doss down in the hay. Once Wowkle has disappeared, the lovers kiss passionately. They are bowled over by each other as is indicated by her fortissimo top C, and Johnson's 'Minnie what a pretty name!'.

But Johnson is clearly worried about something: he is edgy, and makes to leave. He tries to goes out into the snow,[12] but the appalling weather drives him back in. The sound of three pistol shots is heard. He declares that he will never leave her: they declare they will live and die together.

11 A reference to the country love-nest in which the lovers would like to settle is a standard Puccini feature, appearing in *Manon*, and *Tosca*; in *Madama Butterfly*, they are already in it.
12 Puccini makes considerable use of a wind-machine in this act.

They start to settle down separately for the night, (a harp playing *più piano possible*), he in the bed, she on the hearth. But he is still very nervous, and thinks he hears people calling. She asks his name. 'Dick'. And she still worries that he he has been with her competitor, Nina Micheltorena. 'Never', he replies.

Nick, the bar tender, interrupts with a knock at the door.[13] Minnie manages to hide Johnson behind a curtain just before Rance, Ashby and Sonora come in. They explain that they were worried about her safety: Ramerrez has been seen; Ramerrez is Johnson. He came to rob the 'Polka' and has been tracked by Nick and Sid (the cheat) nearly as far as Minnie's cabin, where the tracks gave out in the snow. Rance advises her to watch out who she dances with in future.

Minnie wonders how they know that Johnson is Ramerrez. She is told that Nina Micheltorena betrayed him. Rance produces a photo of Johnson which Nina gave them. 'He's her lover', says Rance. Minnie tries to laugh it off. Nick is surprised to find a cigar butt on the floor.

When they have left, Minnie rounds on Johnson and accuses him of coming to rob her. Yes, he is Ramerrez. She is about to turn him out. He describes his childhood. After his father, also a bandit, died six months previously, he was left to provide for the family. When he saw Minnie originally, he had immediately fallen for her. He longed then to go and start life again, but he is in a hopeless situation having to look after the family.

She forgives him for being a bandit, but reproaches him bitterly for taking her first kiss. She braces herself and sends him off. *È finita*, it's all over.

He goes out, suicidally. A shot is heard. She pulls him back in. She loves him, and, despite his protests, pushes him up into the loft.

Rance enters the cabin. When Minnie addresses him as Jack, he ticks her off: he is the sheriff, not Jack. Johnson was shot and cannot now escape. He wants to hear that she does not love Johnson. He tries to kiss, even to rape, her, but she repels him with a whisky bottle and a C sharp. Rance swears that Johnson will never have her. But, as he holds out his hand, drops of blood (the drips depicted by a solo harp) fall from the ceiling onto it. He looks up. The wounded Johnson must be above in the loft. He calls him down, and he offers him a choice between the rope and the gun. But Johnson faints.

---

13 The static effect of the love duet is counteracted by this theatrical interruption.

Minnie claims that they are all thieves and gamblers together: she runs a gambling joint, living on whisky and gold. So she offers a deal. They should play poker. If Rance wins, he can have Johnson and her; if he loses she will have herself and Johnson. Rance, increasingly consumed by his lust for her, agrees.

When she goes to get the cards, she stuffs a couple of them in her stocking. The orchestra complements her action. They then play the best of three. The thumping double basses underpin the feeling of tension. She wins the first hand, but loses the second. When Rance shows three kings in the final hand, she pretends to faint; and while Rance gets the whisky and a glass to revive her, she extracts the winning cards from her stocking and changes the cards. Showing three aces and a pair, she wins the hand. Rance goes off in a fury; Minnie's breaks out into hysterical laughter: *È mio,* 'He's mine'. She embraces the inert Johnson and the curtain falls.

Act 3 A clearing in the great Californian Forest at early dawn in winter
The scene is set about a week later, in the Californian forest among the gigantic trees, not far from Minnie's hut. The double basses play the sinister augmented fourth, the tritone. When the curtain rises, Rance is shown brooding in the cold, obsessed by jealousy. With him are Nick and Ashby. The music is full of whole-tone sounds. They have not caught Johnson yet. Rance, who stood by his part of the bargain with Minnie, kept his word of honour and did not reveal where Johnson was. Now, he pictures him in Minnie's arms. What can the lovely Minnie possibly see in Johnson, he wonders. That's love, suggests Nick, and Minnie[14] has caught the disease badly.

Johnson has made a run for it. The chase continues nearby, led by Ashby. Rance, the rejected suitor, remains behind with Nick. He takes no delight in the chase: after all, Minnie seriously loves Johnson.

Johnson is almost caught, but gets away. However, like a wolf set-upon by hounds, he eventually is captured.

The lynch-mob of gold-diggers, singing their folksong refrain 'Dooda, Dooda Day', relish the prospect of using Johnson for target practice as he swings. When they have rushed off to where he has been captured, Billy, the Native, organises a rope. But Nick, before heading off in the other direction, bribes Billy and warns him to delay using the noose, or he will shoot him.

14 The orchestra reminds us, very quietly and expressively, of the theme associated with Minnie.

84

Ashby hands the defiant Johnson over to Rance, the representative of justice, and rides off, his job done. Rance relishes destroying his rival. He blows the smoke of a cigar in Johnson's face. The gold-diggers accuse Johnson of various murders, but, although he admits to having been a thief, he has never been a murderer. Well, maybe he was not a murderer, but he nearly robbed them. Indeed, he has robbed them of Minnie. The gold-diggers take him to the noose.

Johnson says he does not mind noose or gun. But he wants to speak of the girl he loves. Rance gives him two minutes; and Sonora insists on his right to speak. In a beautiful aria, all too brief, with, as Rance warns, a minute left to go, Johnson explains that he does not want her to know how he died. Let her just think he has gone far off away to live the better life that she has taught him to lead, *Ch'ella mi creda libero e lontano*. Rance is furious and hits him in the face. (This became a popular song with the Italian army in World War I.)

Just as he has finished and is about to be hanged, Minnie gallops in on her pony, pistol between her teeth, followed by Nick. Rance is desperate to complete the execution. But Minnie places herself with her gun in front of Johnson, and despite a scuffle, prevents Rance and the lynch-mob from hanging him. When Rance invokes Justice, she taunts him with being a bad example of that. She, with the orchestra blasting out her theme, says nobody will dare hang Johnson. Realising that he has lost, Rance goes berserk, consumed with rage and his thirst for revenge. But nobody pays him any attention any more.

They try to stop Minnie, and two armed men seize her. But Sonora intervenes on her behalf.

She claims that she has given her best years for the gold-diggers. They did not tell her to stop when she looked after them, *Non vi fu mai chi disse 'Basta'*. She claims Johnson as hers: she had converted the sinner; he was going off to lead a new life. 'I claim him as mine, mine from God', *Ora quest'uomo è mio com'è di Dio!* She goes round each of them and reminds them what she has done for them, for example, when, in a fever, Harry had thought that she was his little sister Maud come from home.

She throws away her pistol. The gold-diggers cave in. Sonora declares that her words must have come from God; her love is divine. On their behalf, he gives Johnson to her.

Together with Johnson, she bids farewell to the dejected, weeping gold-diggers; and she thanks Nick particularly warmly. They ride off into the distance. Goodbye, my sweet earth, goodbye, my California! Beautiful mountains and snows! ... *Addio, mia dolce terra, addio, mia California*. This may be sentimental, over the top, but 'it sure is' effective.

In the US with Gatti-Casazza (who ran La Scala and the Met),
Belasco (playwright), and Toscanini (the conductor)

Il Trittico
(Il Tabarro,
Suor Angelica and
Gianni Schicchi)

CONTENTS

Readers focussed on only one or two of the three operas may find it sufficient to read '*Il Trittico*: Background'; and, in the rest of the Short Guide, omit items which are obviously non-applicable from the title of each section

The summary of the life of Puccini and the view expressed on his place as a composer, on pages 159-163, are very relevant to all three operas

IL TRITTICO : BACKGROUND

At the time of the *Tosca* première, as the nineteenth century turned to the twentieth, Puccini had toyed with the idea of writing three contrasting one-act operas for performance on the same evening. He then envisaged using episodes from Dante's three-part *The Divine Comedy*, a pocket edition of which he tended to read on train journeys.[1]

But the project took about eighteen years to come to fruition in the form of the three one-act operas which were performed collectively in 1918 as *Il Trittico*, the Triptych.[2] Only the third, the hilarious *Gianni Schicchi* (pronounced 'Janny Skeeky'), is based on the *Inferno*, where Dante briefly sees an impersonator undergoing eternal punishment for the crime which the opera portrays.

Puccini had long thought of composing a comic opera. The well-tried story of fortune-seeking relatives scheming to enrich themselves from a rich man's estate had been around for centuries. It harks back to the fairground, strolling players, the *commedia dell'arte*.[3] It had been used by several writers and in opera buffa; and, for example, in Ben Johnson's *Volpone* of around 1600.

The use of a one-act comedy as a foil for earlier horrific material derived from the very successful 'Grand Guignol' theatre which Puccini had encountered in Paris. The effect of the comedy is to enhance the impact of the already contrasting operas which precede it. Whereas *Il Tabarro (The Cloak)* depicts a violent 'crime passionnel' on a barge in Paris, the all-female *Suor Angelica* is set in an Italian convent, in an intentionally sentimental atmosphere. Taken on its own, with its potent concoction of religion and the fallen woman, it can perhaps be too moving, too insipid.

The three operas together are very effective. But with each component lasting around an hour, the evening was long. Very soon, the sensational and the sentimental were cast aside. With the occasional exception, only the comical *Gianni Schicchi*, with its famous 'best-tune' *O mio babbino caro*, lasted in the regular repertoire.

Gianni Schicchi has been called 'the last supreme example of Italian

---

1 *The Divine Comedy* by Dante Alighieri (1265-1321), the eminent Italian poet, comprises the *Inferno (Hell)*, the *Purgatorio* and the *Paradiso*.
2 There is no particular significance in Puccini's title. In the absence any better suggestion, *Il Trittico*, 'The Triptych', 'The Trilogy', seemed to him appropriate for three one-act operas which are related to each other.
3 The parts fit the *commedia dell'arte* mould, with Gianni as a Harlequin, Lauretta as a Columbine and Simone as Pantaloon.

operatic humour'. It has been compared to Verdi's *Falstaff*, a somewhat far-fetched comparison given both scale and achievement. The fun in *Gianni Schicchi* 'lies more in the action than in the musical characterisation', the music being clever rather than great. But, as entertainment, it is uproarious.

Puccini took immense trouble with his choice of libretti. Like Mozart, he appreciated how much operatic success depends on getting that choice right. He learnt this lesson painfully, early in his career, when his *Edgar* flopped. The small number of Puccini's operas, twelve, if one counts each of the *Il Trittico* components as three, is evidence of his diligence. They compare with (say) the seventy operas of Donizetti. Puccini's thoroughness and his concern to get a perfect libretto led to a frantic search. Unfortunately, Giuseppe Giacosa, who with Luigi Illica had provided his earlier successful librettos, was dead. Puccini received many suggestions from his contacts, which included the playwright George Bernard Shaw.

Puccini turned to Forzano, a journalist, playwright and producer. He wanted him to start by providing a libretto based on a horror story which he had recently seen in a play in Paris. Forzano was only prepared to develop his own plots, and refused to do adaptations of existing plays. But he provided Puccini with the idea and the libretti for *Suor Angelica* and *Gianni Schicchi*. The libretto for the first component, *Il Tabarro*, 'The Cloak' was written by Giuseppe Adami, a prolific, if rather lightweight, playwright and librettist. Puccini worked at it on and off, and finished composing it in November 1916.

The Librettists

Giovacchino Forzano (1884–1970) had studied medicine and law. He was later caught up with the Fascists, for whom he organised film propaganda, and with Mussolini himself, with whom he collaborated on three plays. Forzano's refusal to base his libretti on existing material facilitated the development of the opera because there was no 'baggage' left over from the previous material to sort out, delete and edit.

Giuseppe Adami (1878–1946) was the librettist of *La Rondine* and *Turandot* and a biographer of Puccini. *Il Tabarro* was based on Didier Gold's long-running play 'La Houppelande', 'The Cloak', which features two murders. It shows that vice is the product of wretched social conditions. The production of Puccini's opera was delayed until *Suor Angelica* and *Gianni Schicchi* were ready.

Puccini then composed the subsequent operas in no more than a year or so. His eyesight at the time was so poor that he composed on paper with widely spaced staves and in pencil. Even before *Gianni Schicchi* was finished (20 April, 1918), opera houses were competing for the première.

Particularly because of the War, it was decided not to stage it in Rome as originally planned, but in New York. So the première on 14 December, 1918 took place at The Metropolitan Opera House. Because of travel difficulties, Puccini could not be present.

The comedy in *Gianni Schicchi* was bound to be a success with the public. However, *Suor Angelica*, which Puccini himself thought was the best of the three operas, was received coolly.

The reception was similar in Rome in the following month and at Covent Garden in 1920. English audiences found the *Il Trittico*, 'intolerably long'. Although *Gianni Schicchi* was called 'a gem, a masterpiece of comic opera', *Il Tabarro*, realistic and violent, was called 'Puccini réchauffé'. *Suor Angelica*, a tear-jerker which the cognoscenti were always likely to consider far too emotional to be good art, was condemned as 'anaemic'. Its Catholicism was bound to grate on Protestant audiences, regardless of its merits. And, after the second London performance, Beecham (in the role of impresario, rather than conductor) decided to drop *Suor Angelica*, which infuriated Puccini.

> Puccini, who had little recent experience of poverty, and none of chastity or obedience, had an ideal means of testing the realism and accuracy of *Suor Angelica*. Surprisingly perhaps, one of his many sisters was a nun. Suor Enrichetta was Mother Superior of a convent at Vicopelago just outside Lucca. He played and sang the work to the nuns, and apparently moved them to tears. A priest whom he had known for years, advised him on the Latin prayer for the Miracle Scene.

Puccini was stung by the poor reception of *Il Trittico*, and suspected that the music had not been considered modern enough. His contemporary, the pianist and composer Ferrucio Busoni, regarded *Il Tabarro* and *Gianni Schicchi* as masterpieces.

Puccini loathed *Il Trittico* being 'brutally torn to pieces'. As already indicated, he had intended the impact of each opera to be reinforced by the contrast depicted in the subsequent one. Unity is subtly provided by the three moving consecutively backwards in time to the seventeenth and thirteenth centuries; and by the dark mood at the start progressing forward to light and to comedy at the end; and also by the underlying social comment, the snobbery, the blatant anti-clericalism.

But he came to accept that the triple bill was too long. *Gianni Schicchi*, severed from the others, went on to be paired with Mascagni's *Cavalleria rusticana* or Leoncavallo's *Pagliacci* (Cav & Pag) both of which were individually immensely successful, even if neither would have had any place in *Il Trittico*. It has also been combined with Rachmaninov's *The Miserly Knight* and even with Richard Strauss's one-act *Salome*, a ferociously violent work which Puccini could hardly stomach.

The role of Gianni was created by Giuseppe de Luca, the baritone who had created Sharpless in *Madama Butterfly*. Others who have taken the role are Geraint Evans and Thomas Allen; and the opera has been directed by Tito Gobbi. Placido Domingo has sung in both *Il Tabarro* and *Gianni Schicchi*.

The recording studio has provided the opportunity for great sopranos of the past to perform the role of Angelica: Lotte Lehmann, Victoria de los Angeles, Mirella Freni, Joan Sutherland, Renata Tebaldi among others.

Who's Who and What's What

This summary is based on the libretto. As mentioned in the Warning at the end of this book, certain directors may amend opera stories to suit their production.

Il Tabarro (The Cloak)

Michele, assisted by his much younger wife **Giorgetta**, operates a Seine river-barge. He is passionate about her. But she has fallen for **Luigi** one of the stevedores being employed to shift the cargo.

It is 1918, 'the present'; it is sunset; the barge is moored in Paris. In the background are two stevedores, the drunken **Tinca the Tench** and **Talpa the Mole**, with **La Frugola** (the 'Rummager'), Talpa's wife. The scene is completed by a **pedlar, seamstresses, and street musicians** including an **organ grinder**.

Giorgetta and Luigi recall their passion on the previous night. They arrange to meet again: she will give the all clear with a lighted match, the flame of their love.

Michele tries to resurrect his wife's love for him, before they lost their child. He would envelop her in his cloak in a loving embrace. Now, he gets no response from her. When she tears herself away, he calls her *Sgualdrina*, a tart, a slut.

Two lovers are heard in the distance. Michele is now a broken man: he lights his pipe. Luigi thinks this is the 'all clear' signal. When he comes aboard, Michele throttles him and wraps the corpse in his cloak. Giorgetta comes up from below: she is remorseful. She sidles up to him. But it is too late. Michele opens his cloak and Luigi's corpse falls out. He shoves her face against that of her dead lover.

Suor Angelica

In total contrast to *Il Tabarro*, we enter a quiet, pleasant but disciplined convent at the end of the seventeenth century. **Sister Angelica** is late for the service which has finished. She was once a princess, but was sent to the convent because she disgraced her family by becoming an unmarried mother.

The convent consists of Sisters, Novices, Lay Sisters and staff from various backgrounds, all ruled by the **Abbess**, who is assisted by the disciplinarian **Sister Zelatrice**, the **Mistress of the Novices**, and the **Head of the Infirmary**. The Sisters include Sister Angelica's particular friends, the naughty and resentful **Osmina**, the good **Genovieffa** (formerly a shepherdess), and the plump **Dolcina**.

Sister Angelica is now in charge of the garden and herbs. She longs to hear news of her child. She has heard nothing of him since, seven years ago, she was confined in the closed order. Other Sisters return from collecting alms, money and food which has been donated.

Unusually, a visitor is allowed in. It is **La Zia Principessa**, The Princess Aunt, Sister Angelica's aunt and guardian. Frigid, awful, she has come to force Angelica to sign away her patrimony to her own sister who is about to get married. Angelica bitterly resents her aunt's total lack of humanity and inability to forgive.

When told that the boy died two years ago, she weeps uncontrollably: *Senza mamma, bimbo, tu sei morto!* But at the thought of Death, she becomes ecstatic. She will join her son in Paradise.

That night, she drinks a concoction of poisonous herbs. She realises, too late, that, as a suicide, she is damned and will never meet her son. She prays desperately to the Madonna for forgiveness. In the final **'Miracle'** scene, the **Virgin** appears with a **small boy**. She motions him towards the dying nun, with whom he is united in Paradise. The Miracle takes place.

Gianni Schicchi

Many centuries earlier, at the deathbed of the rich Florentine patrician **Buoso** Donati, his **Relatives** are aghast. **Betto**, an impecunious brother-in-law, reports that he has heard that the monks are due to inherit the lot. The deceased's elderly cousin, Simone, advises them[4] to find Buoso's will, urgently. They are horrified to discover that the rumour is right. They are disinherited and impoverished. They must do something about it.

The young and forward-looking **Rinuccio**, who finds the will, claims a reward. He has been hoping to marry **Lauretta** his twenty-one year-old girl-friend. He hopes that the foregathering at the deathbed, plus a bequest, could provide a suitable opportunity and justification for seeking the necessary consent from his snobbish aunt **Zita**, another cousin of the deceased. However, she regards Lauretta as totally 'unsuitable', being merely the daughter of **Gianni Schicchi**, an upstart, a joker with a 'common', prominent nose. But Rinuccio sends for him, because he is adept at finding solutions to problems such as legal ones.

When Gianni arrives, he, Zita and Rinuccio hurl insults at each other, while the other Relatives just want to resolve the matter of the will.

---

4 The Relatives also include Buoso's nephew, Gherardo, Nella his wife and their small son Gherardino; and Simone's son Marco and his wife La Ciesca.

Pretending to be persuaded by Lauretta's pleas (in **O mio babbino caro**), Gianni arranges to provide the solution by impersonating Buoso.

Fortunately nobody outside the room is aware that Buoso has expired. They heave his corpse out of the way into an adjacent room.

They are interrupted by **Maestro Spinelloccio**, the doctor. But, by imitating Buoso's voice, Gianni gets him to push off, and also demonstrates his own skill as an impersonator. Then the Relatives are horrified to hear the bell toll for the dead – it's too late! but that is a false alarm – it tolls for someone else.

Gianni gets them to reveal the plum items in the estate, (the house, the best mule in Tuscany, and the mill). To avoid squabbling, they leave it up to him to decide to whom these should be bequeathed. He warns them that impersonation in wills is punishable by the hand being chopped off prior to exile: *Addio Firenze*. (It follows that, once the Relatives are implicated in the fraud, they cannot safely object to anything he does.)

Buoso (Gianni) dictates the will to the notary **Ser Amantio di Nicolao**, who is accompanied by two witnesses, **Pinellino**, the cobbler, and **Guccio**, the dyer. He leaves the plum items to...himself. When the Relatives expostulate, Gianni sings echoes of *Addio Firenze*, and waves a seemingly handless stump.

The Relatives are driven out of what is now Gianni's house, leaving behind only Rinuccio and Lauretta, who will now be the heiress to a rich father. Gianni, pointing to them, suggests that, if the audience has been amused, it will hopefully accept a plea of 'mitigating circumstances' in relation to his crime.

TALKING POINTS

Giacomo Puccini (1858–1924)
Please see the summary of the life of Puccini on pages 159 and 160.

Puccini's Place as a Composer – a View
The view expressed on pages 161-163 is very relevant.

Dante and the real Gianni Schicchi
Gianni Schicchi dei Cavalcanti, a well known mimic in Florence, died around 1280, when Dante was about fifteen. He impersonated Buoso di Vinciguerra, the recently deceased father of his friend Simone Donati,[5] in order to secure for him a major portion of the estate. Much to the fury of Simone, Gianni also inherited Buoso's valuable mare.

Gianni is referred very briefly in the Thirtieth Canto of the *Inferno*, being the first section of Dante's *The Divine Comedy*. Dante was led through the Inferno by Virgil, the Latin poet. Deep down, in the Tenth Chasm of the Eighth Circle, they found Gianni Schicchi in a place reserved for falsifiers. He was with the mythical Myrrha, the mother of Adonis, who had disguised herself in order to copulate with her father. (Later, she was transformed into a myrrh tree whose aroma is generated by her tears.) Both characters, 'lifeless and naked', in the guise of demented demons, were condemned to run around naked, 'like pigs let out of a sty', sinking their fangs into everything in sight.

Dante calls the mare which Gianni acquired 'the lady of the company', clearly a thoroughbred. In the opera libretto, the mare is demoted to a mule, a subtlety probably lost on many listeners.

Aside from Gianni's fraud and forgery, any impersonation or falsification of ones identity, as in acting, was thoroughly disapproved of by the State and by the Church which regarded it as a sin. As far back as Roman times, actors suffered the stigma of 'infamia', loss of social standing and of the legal protection provided by the State. Emperor Tiberius prohibited them from having any contact with the upper classes. Even centuries later, Molière, the French playwright and actor, was an excommunicate and had to be buried at dead of night.

---

5 Dante's wife came from the Donati family.

One-act operas

The three one-act operas making up *Il Trittico* sounded the 'last echo' of a trend which began thirty years earlier, when a publisher arranged a competition for a one-act opera. Mascagni's *Cavalleria rusticana* was a winner and this became a trail blazer for Leoncavallo's *Pagliacci*.

The success of these two may be attributed to their dealing realistically with the earthy emotions which are so successful on the stage, sex, violence, betrayal and retribution. With origins in Bizet's *Carmen*, and perhaps earlier in Verdi's *La Traviata*, characters are 'swept along in a whirlwind of passion'. Thwarted sex becomes the driving force, and 'leads to acts of insensate jealousy and savage revenge'. These acts are 'almost invariably committed on the open stage so as to score a direct hit at the spectator's sensibility'. Because excessive tension cannot be sustained for too long, the one-act opera became the ideal form for this. The analogy with an episode in a TV series is obvious.

Verismo and Grand Guignol

The Realism, 'Verismo' of *Il Tabarro* follows a tradition to which various painters had adhered for many decades. In opera, it reflected the naturalistic epoch in literature, such as is found in the relentlessly realistic novels of Emile Zola, whose aim was 'to register human facts, to lay bare the mechanism of body and soul'.

With its 'tenebrous' atmosphere rising from the river, *Il Tabarro*, has been described as 'outstanding for its painting of a sombre atmosphere and its dramatic concentration'. Puccini told its librettist to portray the harsh reality, warts and all, of working on the 'murky Seine against the background of Notre Dame'.

In the very successful 'Grand Guignol' theatre in Paris which had its hey-day in the first half of the twentieth century, the primary feature of the show was a highly realistic horror story such as this. The comedy which followed it provided the contrast.

Listening to a disc of *Il Tabarro* and *Suor Angelica* is sufficient – the music tells the story. *Il Tabarro* leaves one gasping. Even though it may be unfashionable, it is hard not to shed a tear at the end of *Suor Angelica*. In both, there is more evocation of atmospheric contrast than portrayal of the characters themselves. This is different from the works of Verdi, for whom character came first, and then atmosphere.

The flaw in the three-opera concept

Unfortunately, three contrasting self-standing operas provide the opportunity to pick and choose. Although it is virtually inconceivable today[6] that one act would be extracted from a three-act full-length opera, the uproarious *Gianni Schicchi* can easily be performed without the other two. That is what has happened. That it was designed as part of a whole, but as a contrast to the other two, is conveniently overlooked. Besides, the other two have come in for a lot of stick.

Even though Puccini intended the story of *Il Tabarro* to be brutal, 'wounding almost', Toscanini (the great conductor) thought that he had gone too far, and that the technicolour was in bad taste.

Equally, the religious, over-emotional atmosphere of *Suor Angelica* – embarrassing even, especially the Miracle – is too mawkish and insufficiently 'PC' to secure its regular live performance today. (For critics to damn its cloistral atmosphere for being too unvaried is to ignore the opera's place in the middle of a trilogy. Nobody needed to teach Puccini about the importance of variety, and the dangers of uniformity. Besides, *Suor Angelica* portrays realistically convent life in the seventeenth century, and probably the early twentieth as well.)

Puccini's publisher Giulio Ricordi, who had a very sure touch for what would succeed, disliked his plan for three contrasting operas, but he died in 1912 long before the work saw the light of day.

Doria and Suor Angelica

Tragic events of a few years earlier weighed heavily on Puccini, and the short operas required less sustained energy than a full opera. An unpleasant event which came to a head in the last few months of 1908 and the beginning of 1909, is thought to have influenced the portrayal of Sister Angelica, her ghastly aunt, and of Liù in *Turandot* (the carer of the Prince's father, who kills herself rather than disclose Prince Calaf's name). It may also have impacted negatively the composition of *La Fanciulla*.

Puccini had kept a mistress, Elvira, for around twenty years. He married her after the death of her husband, in 1904. But he became bored with her: she had not kept pace with his success. He was a notorious womaniser. Elvira became desperately jealous. She found him late at night chatting to the twenty-one year-old Doria Manfredi, one of the domestic servants, at his house in Torre del Lago, near Lucca. Elvira became hysterical and started following Doria around the village, shrieking abuse. Doria was driven to committing an agonising suicide by drinking poison.

---

6 There are exceptions: act 2 of Rossini's *Guillaume Tell*, a very long opera, was performed separately in the decade after its performance.

After this, Doria's family prosecuted Elvira, who was convicted, fined and sentenced to several months in jail. The case was settled at great cost to the maestro, so Elvira was not imprisoned. Not surprisingly, the whole matter caused Puccini enormous worry.

O mio babbino caro (Gianni Schicchi)

O mio babbino caro, 'Dear Daddy', is one of Puccini's 'Best Tunes' and has been known to be sung at weddings. There is of course no guarantee that, at the signing of the register, the bickering will be less confrontational than has just been heard in *Gianni Schicchi*.

However, by that stage at a wedding, the father has already given the bride away. So it is too late for him to object (as if he could, these days!). Therefore she is unlikely to throw herself into the river (as her aria implies she might do).

Today, the choice of wedding music often has little regard to its operatic origin. The exit of the bride to the Grand March from *Aïda*, which features elephants and more ferocious wild animals, is another hilariously inappropriate example.

ACT BY ACT

Il Tabarro (The Cloak)

The score specifies that the curtain is raised before the music begins. The first impression – contemporary Paris at sunset, on a Seine river barge – is thus visual. The barge owner, the fifty year-old Michele, stares into the sunset; his wife Giorgetta (half his age), does her chores. The men (stevedores) can be heard down below, shifting the cargo.

The music opens with the River theme, evocating the darkness of the water. We hear the sound of tugboat siren and whistle, and the distant sound of a car horn. Giorgetta suggests that the stevedores should be given a drink, cool wine. Although Michele's pipe has burnt out, his passion for her has not. He wants a kiss. She rejects his advances, 'offering her cheek instead of her lips'; he goes off down into the hold.

Giorgetta is enamoured of Luigi, one of the stevedores, aged twenty. She offers him a drink; and also offers one to Il Tinca (known as the Tench) and to Il Talpa (the Mole). Luigi hails the organ grinder on the quay, and with the 'organetto' playing deliberately out of tune[7] and wrongly, Giorgetta makes a move to dance with Luigi, but Tinca gets in first. They dance clumsily, to everyone's amusement. She escapes into the arms of Luigi. At this moment, Michele arrives and converses sourly with his wife. Street musicians ('Vendors of Songs') play music and the midinettes (seamstresses) listen and buy a song off a pedlar. The pedlar, playing a small harp, sings of the transitory nature of love, how those who have lived for love, like Mimì, (with a quote from *La Bohème*) die for it.[8]

As the sun drenched in blood, sinks on the silent river, Giorgetta regrets the passing of summer. Tinca's wife La Frugola[9] arrives with a sack of items, bric-a-brac of all varieties, which she has collected. (She also has food for her cat, who keeps her company while her husband is out.) She upbraids Tinca for getting drunk. He says it anaesthetises the hard work. Luigi echoes this and the hard life they lead: every joy turns to sorrow.

La Frugola just wants a nice little house in the country in which to settle

---

7 The out of tune impression is achieved by the orchestra playing in sevenths rather than in octaves.

8 This theme runs through Puccini's works: life-enhancing love is inseparable with death, which is life destroying; love has to be atoned for by death. The heroine's guilty true love has to be punished by physical or mental suffering which grinds her relentlessly down to death. The male is usually the catalyst, or the persecutor in this process, although in *Suor Angelica* it is the aunt who fulfils this role. Turandot is another female persecutor.

9 Considering she is a minor part, she is given a large amount of singing to do.

down. Giorgetta however longs to stop her life on the barge and to enjoy the highlife of Belleville, that part of enchanting, smiling, spellbound Paris from which Luigi also comes. She wants picnics in the country, with the sound of the cuckoo.[10] Talpa and Frugola go off to eat, and singers are heard in the background rounding off the first part of the opera with the opening theme of the Seine, and a tugboat whistle in the background.

Puccini has painted the scene. There is a pause. Now for the action. The increasingly sombre mood of the second half contrasts with the relatively light first half. Giorgetta, using a recurring triplet love theme, warns Luigi to be careful because Michele might appear at any moment – if he knew, he would kill them both. They recall last night and their kisses. Michele does appear and Luigi asks him to drop him off when they sail through Rouen, although Michele warns him that he will get no work there.

Michele goes to prepare the lights, leaving the lovers together.[11] This is not a moment for a love song: it is time for raw passion. Giorgetta wonders why Luigi wants to go to Rouen: it is because he cannot bear to share her with Michele. The moment when he takes her, 'quando tu mi prendi', she breathlessly tells him, compensates for every feeling of guilt. They embrace and exchange 'baci senza fine', kisses without end. But he suddenly suspects that he hears Michele in the background as the orchestra makes obvious. They arrange to meet: she will give the all-clear with a lighted match, the flame of their love. He cannot wait, and she has to resist his ardour and force him to rush off.

Just in time. Michele comes from the cabin and wonders if she is going to bed. She says that he was right to retain Luigi. But there is not enough work for all of them. When she suggests that he fires Tinca, who is always drunk, Michele menacingly points out that he drinks to drown his sorrows; otherwise he would strangle his wife, who is a tart.

In a scene in which the orchestra evokes the mood in a masterly way, Michele asks Giorgetta why she does not love him anymore. Her answers are dissonant. He recalls their shared life together, moments of sorrow and happiness; in particular, the baby who died last year. Previously, drifting along in the boat, he would envelop her in his cloak in a loving embrace: *Vi raccoglievo insieme nel tabarro come in una carezza*. His grey hair is now an insult to her youthfulness. But he knows why she will not sleep tonight. Desperately, he makes a last attempt to persuade her to stay with him: *Resta vicino a me! La notte è bella*. But things have moved

---

10 Puccini, who was a keen wildfowler, includes birds in most of his operas. The opening of *Suor Angelica* has a bird replicated by the piccolo off stage.
11 The excitement of the drama can easily distract from the way in which Puccini's music enhances this episode.

on. The church bell tolls the hour. When she tears herself away, he calls her 'Sgualdrina', a tart, a slut.

Two lovers are heard in the distance; and a bugle is heard from the barracks. Michele ponders the situation: *Nulla! Silenzio!*[12] He can see that she has not gone to bed, and is waiting. He tortures himself wondering who has come between them: Talpa is too old; Tinca drinks. He pauses a moment. Luigi? That's improbable:[13] he spoke as if he meant to get off at Rouen. Michele longs to drag whoever it is down with him into the black abyss. He cries out in anguish (on top G), 'Peace is in Death', *La pace è nella morte.* Totally broken, he takes his pipe and lights it.

Luigi thinks the light is the 'all clear' signal. When he boards the barge, Michele grabs him by the throat, and tells him to confess. Luigi tries to get him with his knife, but Michele tells him he will flow down to Rouen in the river, dead. He throttles him as he makes him confess that he loves Giorgetta.

Michele wraps the corpse in his cloak.

Giorgetta emerges frightened and remorseful. She sidles up to him. Doesn't he want her any more? Where, in my cloak? *Dove? Nel mio Tabarro?* Yes, close, in his cloak which in the past he has said 'sometimes hides sorrow, sometimes joy'. This time, he warns, it conceals a crime. He opens it and Luigi's corpse falls out. His wife screams and tries to get away. He seizes her and pushes her face down into that of her dead lover. The orchestra concludes 'tutta forza' and 'selvaggio', savagely.

Suor Angelica
We have moved backwards in time. In total contrast, it is the end of the seventeenth century, by the fountain in a convent where the service, the *Ave Maria*, has started.[14] Birds can be heard singing (on the piccolo, offstage). Sister Angelica was late for Divine Office and kneels and kisses the ground by way of contrition. Two lay Sisters do not. After the end of the Office, the Abbess and the nuns emerge. Sister Zelatrice, the monitor, issues a penance to them and to other Sisters who have misbehaved: one giggled; and Sister Osmina had two roses concealed in her sleeve. Sister

12 *Nulla Silenzio* has been compared with some of Verdi's great baritone and bass arias. Puccini replaced an earlier aria *Scorri, fiume eterno*, which is sometimes put at the end. In this, Michele contemplates the water of the Seine. It will wash away his suffering as it carries him to his death.
13 The orchestra recalls the triplet love theme from the lover's first duet (when she warns Luigi to be careful).
14 Puccini's portrayal of detail, 'little unimportant things in the lives of little unimportant people', is notable in the first half of this opera.

Osmina resentfully slams the door of her cell. Zelatrice then sends the Sisters off to work. Angelica tends her flowers.

Sister Genovieffa draws attention to the sunshine on the fountain: on three evenings a year, the sunshine in May makes the water appear gilded; she praises and thanks Our Lady for this (apparent) miracle. She is reminded of the passage of time, and that, since last year, one of their number has died. Genovieffa suggests that they take some of the golden water for the flowers on the dead nun's grave: she would certainly have wished it.

Angelica suggests that wishes do not bloom in the Valley of Death: *I desideri sono i fiori dei vivi*. There is no need: the Virgin Mother anticipates them. *La morte è vita bella*, Death is a beautiful Life. This leads to a discussion of wishing. Genovieffa, who was once a shepherdess, longs to see a lamb which she has not seen for five years (a bleating sound, five notes falling, is repeated several times in the orchestra). Another, the plump Sister Dolcina, just wishes for some nice food.

Sister Angelica pretends that she has no wish. And the nuns accuse her of lying, because she wants to see her family of whom she has not heard for seven years. She, once a princess, had been confined to a convent as punishment.

Suddenly, some nun is stung by a wasp and Angelica, who has great skill in the use of herbs and flowers, provides a curative herb. She says that the stung Sister must not moan, because moaning just increases the pain.

Immediately after Angelica says that she is pleased to have been able to help, we hear the orchestra imitate a donkey's raucous 'he-haw': two lay-Sisters have been collecting alms and are returning with a donkey laden with donations. Dolcina is particularly pleased with the raspberries. (The juxtaposition of an ass, a symbol of ignorance and stupidity, enhances the irony that these nuns depend on charity to finance their unproductive activity.)

One of them says that a carriage has been seen at the front door. They all hope the visitor is for them. This agitates Angelica. A bell is heard. The Abbess arrives to call Angelica, whose aunt, the princess, has come to see her. Angelica has long been waiting and praying for news; the Abbess ticks her off for being overwrought. The other nuns leave to take water from the fountain to the cemetery where they can be heard singing the Requiem. The Abbess admonishes Angelica that in the parlatory, she should only say as much as obedience requires. Every word is heard by the Virgin.

Her aunt enters limping on her ebony stick.[15] She does not even greet Angelica; she is as frigid as possible and largely ignores her. She became her guardian after her father and mother died twenty years ago. They willed that she divide the patrimony, which is what she now has done. She has used her power to amend the division, in the event of a fault or indiscretion. She has a document for Angelica to sign – she can read it, discuss it, sign it. Angelica observes that she is now in this holy place. Surely it is a place of pity and love. 'Of penitence', snorts the aunt.

Angelica must renounce all her claims, for ever. Her sister Anna Viola, who was but a child when Angelica last saw her seven years ago, is to be married. 'Who is to dress her?', Angelica asks hopefully. But it is not to be her. She is to be attended by a family member who forgave Angelica's sin which had stained the family reputation. Angelica begins to respond resentfully, and calls her mother's sister *inesorabile*, inexorable. Her aunt is furious and describes how in the family oratory, she communicates with Angelica's dead mother, who calls for *Espiare*, expiation.

Angelica says that she has offered everything to the Virgin, but one thing she cannot give up is her memory of her child, who was torn away from her. She wants to hear of the baby who she saw and kissed but once, her child, *creatura mia*! – of whom she has not heard for seven years. (Her hysteria at this moment is represented in the orchestra, at *Figlio mio*, by the repetition eighteen times of the same single bar theme.)

At first, the aunt is silent; Angelica warns her, with a discordant outburst, that the Virgin is judging her too. The princess tells her coldly and impassively that the boy died two years ago. At this, Angelica is overcome with sorrow, and collapses. The libretto tells us that the aunt thinks that she has fainted and makes a move to assist; but after she sees that she has not done so, she restrains any sign of pity, and stands before an image and prays. Other nuns come with a paper and writing materials. Angelica signs the parchment and the aunt, haughtily as ever, leaves, after giving her niece a final glance.

After this, Angelica weeps uncontrollably. The score is marked 'Andante desolato', for her terrible lament. The child died without its mother, or knowing how much she loved him: *Senza mamma, bimbo, tu sei morto!* Now he is dead, he will be able to hover around and be with her. When will she be able to join him in heaven? *Parlami*, speak to me (on top A), she pleads. At the thought of it, Death, she becomes ecstatic. Other nuns return and marvel that the Virgin has obviously shown her Grace. She is happy (on top C)! The sound of the clappers calls the nuns to their cells. There is a beautiful intermezzo.

15 Puccini has the artistic sense to rely on the drama of the stage action at this stage, and his musical accompaniment is incidental. Verdi once wrote: 'There are moments in the theatre when poets and composers must have the talent to write neither poetry nor music'.

It is night. Angelica emerges and, expert as she is with flowers and herbs, she heats up a concoction of poisonous herbs. She bids farewell. (Puccini cut another aria which he had composed for her at this moment.) She has been called by her son to Paradise.

But having drunk the poison, she rapidly comes to her senses, and realises that, as a suicide, she is damned. She shrieks *Ah! son dannata!* She desperately beseeches the Madonna for forgiveness, for a sign of Grace: *Dammi un segno di grazia, Madonna, Salvami!*

Reaching high C, in what has been called an 'expression of pasteboard religiosity', entitled 'The Miracle', *Il Miracolo*, Suor Angelica hears the voice of angels. The chapel shines with light, and the Virgin, 'La Regina del Conforto, Madre della Madri', appears with a beautiful, fair-haired child in front of her, *un bimbo biondo*. Without touching him, the Madonna gestures the child towards the dying nun, with whom he is united in death. The scene is transfigured: in the words of the libretto, *Il miracolo sfolgora*.

For this deeply moving conclusion – whatever ones point of view – the orchestra is supplemented by an offstage celestial orchestra with, inter alia, two pianos, and organ and three trombones.

Gianni Schicchi

Although we are in Florence around 1299 at the death bed of the rich patrician Buoso Donati, the opera starts with a bang, a contrast to the religious and emotional pianissimo that concludes *Suor Angelica*. Buoso's Relatives[16] stand beside his bedside: *Povere Buoso*. That is, apart from Gherardino, the small great-nephew of the dying man, who is fooling around, and whose father Gherardo takes him away.

Betto, an impecunious brother-in-law, reports that it is rumoured in Signa[17] that Buoso has left everything to the monks. The Relatives ask the elderly cousin Simone for advice. He observes that, if the monks already have the will, it is hopeless; but if the will is to be found in that room, there is a chance...and they all scurry to search for it. Betto tries to use the diversion to help himself to the silver, but is interrupted.

---

16 Unusually, the ages of the protagonists are prescribed in the score. Lauretta (21) is the daughter of Gianni (50). Buoso's cousin Zita (60) is the aunt of Rinuccio (24). The other cousin Simone, aged 70, has a son Marco, aged 45, who is married to La Ciesca, aged 38. Buoso has a nephew Gherardo (40) who has a wife Nella (34), and they have a son Gherardino (7). The age of Betto de Signa, brother-in-law, is indeterminable.
17 Signa is a few miles to the west of Florence, in the direction of Puccini's birthplace in Lucca.

Rinnucio, the nephew of Buoso's cousin Zita, desperately needs a bequest so that he can marry Lauretta, the twenty-one year-old daughter of Gianni Schicchi, a 'nouveau riche' with a 'commonly' prominent nose. Rinnucio finds the will, and, as a reward, claims permission from Aunt Zita (note the link with *Suor Angelica*) to marry her. Rinuccio tells Gherardino to rush and fetch Lauretta and her father.

At first, there are no scissors to cut the ribbon on the will, because Betto has pinched them. They read the will *'Ai miei cugini Zita e Simone'*... With the hope that this inspires, Simone lights the candles. But it is a false hope and Simone extinguishes the candles. Increasingly horrified, they explode as they realise that all the valuable things have indeed been left to the Church: *Dunque era vero*. They picture the monks laughing, as they fatten themselves, at their, the Donati family's, expense. Hysteria turns to depression.

They wonder whether there is any way of changing the will, *E non c'è nessun mezzo*, and they look to Simone, the eldest, for advice. But he despairs. Then, Rinuccio suggests that they ask Gianni Schicchi. Led by Zita, they explode at the very thought of this peasant with a nose like a tower on its side. They don't intend to let a Donati marry the daughter of an upstart.[18] Rinuccio accuses them of prejudice. Gianni is clever, and Florence needs new blood, he explains. Gianni may be a peasant; but, as he points out with great nationalistic pomposity, the City of Florence draws on emigrants from the country around it for its life-blood. He cites Giotto, the painter, Arnolfo, the architect of the cathedral, and even the Medici. Long live Gianni Schicchi!

At this suitable moment, as the music redolent of a march by Elgar reaches its climax, there is a knock at the door, and the comical Gianni (having been fetched by Gherardino), arrives. He observes all the sorry looks: *Quale aspetto sgomento e desolato*. He comes out with some platitudes suited to the occasion. But when he mentions 'you lose a relative but gain an inheritance', Zita explodes and tells him to get out: she is not having her nephew marry a girl without a dowry. 'Stingy bitch', replies Gianni.

Zita, Gianni and Rinuccio argue furiously over whether there can now be a marriage, and they hurl insults at each other. Meanwhile, the other Relatives just want to talk about the will. Rinuccio pleads for Gianni to help them, but *Niente!* – to dissonances on the horns, trombones and bassoons – he totally rejects the idea of helping such frightful people.

---

18 Dante deplored the way in which the 'nouveaux riches' have become proud and their behaviour immoderate.

In complete contrast to the dissonances, and to a rolling harp accompaniment, Lauretta pleads with him in the famous aria: *O mio babbino caro*, Oh Daddy dear, he's gorgeous! I'm off to the Via Porta Rossa to buy the Ring. If you don't give Permission, I'll throw myself into the Arno from the Ponte Vecchio; I'm so tormented I just want to die. Mercy, mercy! (Puccini marked the tempo *andantino ingenuo* and wanted Lauretta to be 'an ingénue, small of figure, fresh of voice, and without any dramatic allure'.)

Pretending to be under duress, Gianni takes the will, *Datemi il testamento!* and then says that the case is hopeless. (Whereupon the couple say farewell to their hopes for a Mayday wedding.) 'However'.... '*Però*'....(And things look up).

The Relatives wait with baited breath. Having got Lauretta to go outside, Gianni checks that, crucially, nobody but nobody, apart from those present, knows that Buoso is actually dead. This is to a percussive accompaniment of cellos, basses and harp playing chords at the bottom of the register. He gets Marco and Gherardo to move the corpse next door.

Everyone is horrified to hear a knock at the door. But, to painful dissonances on the woodwind, they discover that it is only the doctor (who has the Bolognese accent appropriate for a doctor).[19] The Relatives stop him coming in: 'he's better', *Va meglio!* They are taken aback to hear the 'corpse' utter – Betto even drops the silver plate which he has filched – as Gianni imitates the voice of the dead man. Maestro Spinelloccio, the doctor, regards the fact that the bowels have moved as another wonder of science, attributable, of course, to research at the ancient University of Bologna. He agrees to Buoso's request (i.e. Gianni's) that he should come back later.

Having checked that the voice sounded OK, *Era uguale la voce?* Gianni outlines his scheme. The notary should be fetched because Buoso wants to make a will: *Ah! Che zucconi!* He, Gianni, will pretend to be Buoso in the bed. The Relatives are absolutely delighted. They discuss the items which they want to be bequeathed, *Ecco la cappelina*. They reveal that the plum items are the house, the mule and the mill at Signa. Simone presumes they all want him to have these, but their outraged protests are interrupted when they hear the bell tolling for the dead. Fortunately it's a false alarm: a servant has had an accident. They decide to allow Gianni to decide who the plum items should go to. Gianni dresses up as the dead man. And they all try to bribe him to leave them what they want. Each thinks that he or she has persuaded him. They get him into the bed.

---

19 Bologna University was once the most celebrated in Italy. Oxford could be the English equivalent, and Spinelloccio might have been expected to have had an Oxford accent.

Gianni warns them that impersonation in wills is punishable with the hand being cut off prior to exile from Florence: *Prima un avvertimento... Addio Firenze*. They are duly impressed and, in unison, echo the warning.

Rinuccio brings in the notary, Ser Amantio di Nicolao, together with two witnesses, Pinellino, the cobbler and Guccio, the dyer: *Ecco il notaro!* Gianni explains that he cannot use his hand any more (a dire warning to the Relatives) and therefore needs the notary to write the will. All show due compassion.

Amantio, the notary, wonders whether the Relatives should be sent out. No, they should remain, says Gianni. Using suitable professional jargon, Amantio declares the preamble to the will: Buoso revokes all previous wills and testaments. He asks about the funeral arrangements which Buoso desires. Very inexpensive, says Gianni, who proceeds to dictate the will, leaving a pittance to the friars – large sums of money left to the church are always deemed to be stolen money. How wise he is! He then leaves various items to the Relatives, and they are duly grateful. But the plum items, one by one (including the mule, the best in Tuscany), he leaves to ....Gianni Schicchi. When they expostulate, Gianni sings echoes of *Addio Firenze*, and waves an apparently handless stump. He will do what he wants.

When the notary and witnesses have gone with appropriate decorum, the Relatives attack Gianni, *'Ladro! Ladro!'* and begin to plunder the house; but he fights back and tells them to get out. They are driven away, leaving only Rinuccio and Lauretta, Gianni's daughter, behind: *Lauretta mia, staremo sempre qui!* The couple recall their first kiss: it was Paradise, *Paradiso*.

Gianni returns and sees them, and suggests to the audience that Buoso's money could not have been used for a better purpose. He landed up in the *Inferno*, but, with Dante's permission, if the audience has been amused (and he duly applauds himself) – *Diteme voi signori* – it will hopefully accept his plea of 'mitigating circumstances'.

Turandot

Puccini in Vienna with Jeritza,
the greatly admired Tosca, Minnie and Turandot

CONTENTS

TURANDOT: BACKGROUND

Puccini's last opera *Turandot* is his 'greatest masterpiece and swansong'. It appears in charts of the top twenty most-performed operas. In particular, the aria *Nessun dorma*, sung by Pavarotti in the role of Calaf, the Unknown Prince, provided one of the most famous recordings in classical music, two-and-a-half minutes of sheer melodic perfection.

Having reached his sixties, Puccini wanted to compose something different, something fantastic. He was not taken with the suggestion of doing an opera based on the story of *Oliver Twist*; so he took up the idea of Renato Simoni, a scholarly author, that he should use *Re Turandote*, a play by Gozzi, the Venetian eighteenth-century dramatist. (See page 113.) Goethe had particularly liked this, and it had already attracted some composers. Seven years earlier, Puccini's contemporary Ferruccio Busoni had composed a two-act opera, and, before that, Carl Maria von Weber had composed incidental music for it. Puccini actually used a version adapted by Schiller, the great German dramatist.

Puccini was most careful in his choice of libretti. He had the genius to see its operatic potential and to create a spectacle which grips audiences and accounts for the success of *Turandot* today.

The ghastly subject matter was a particularly improbable choice for the great womaniser Puccini. Gozzi's message is anti-feminist: male weakness allows female insubordination, and results in social disorder. Gozzi depicts the havoc caused by a stunningly beautiful Chinese Princess, 'the ultimate castrating female', who so abhors men that she gets the Emperor, her utterly pathetic father, to enact virtually certain decapitation for any man foolish enough to aspire to possess her: if the suitor fails to give the right answer to three virtually impossible riddles, his head will be chopped off, instantly.

The tale probably originates in The Arabian Nights, or earlier, and can also be found in the cultural heritage of many societies. In *The Nibelungenlied*, a source for Wagner's *Ring*, suitors for Brunhild, a lady of 'vast strength and surpassing beauty', had to beat her at three tests, throwing the javelin, hurling a weight, and at the long-jump. Failure at even one test would cost the suitor his life. In Shakespeare's *The Merchant of Venice*, each of the suitors for the hand of Portia had to choose from three caskets, having first sworn, if he makes the wrong choice, 'never to speak to lady afterward, in way of marriage' – a less extreme fate.

With Simoni, himself an expert on Gozzi, and Giuseppe Adami, who had written the libretti for his less successful operas *La Rondine* and *Il*

Tabarro, Puccini masterminded a libretto, a mixture of tragedy, grotesque comedy and 'the fantastications of a fairy-tale'.

Puccini had been concerned that he was growing out of touch with modern music. He told Simoni at one stage, 'Nobody sings in Italy any longer. Instead there are crashes, discordant chords ...' The exotic setting, and Turandot's horrible character, justified him in imparting modern, dissonant and exotic sounds which we might not otherwise expect, or like, from him. How he succeeded! Emotionally (not least in his creation of the slave girl Liù), he carries his audience, which might reasonably be disgusted, along with him. His music makes dramatically convincing some otherwise wholly incredible and dislikable protagonists. And peeping out among his frequently angular and shrill sounds, is melody which lingers in the mind, and which we hum, as we leave the theatre.

Puccini never saw *Turandot*, which he spent the last four years of his life struggling to compose. The première, conducted by the legendary Arturo Toscanini, was in Milan at La Scala on 25 April, 1926, seventeen months after his death from throat cancer. He had only completed the score up to the death of Liù, the slave girl, in the final act.

At the time when he departed for the clinic in Brussels where he died, he left behind various sketches and thirty-six pages of continuous music in 'short score' indicating how the opera was to close. These were used by the unfortunate Franco Alfano to construct and compose a conclusion to the opera. Toscanini gave him a hard time. At first, he rejected his work and then he cut it drastically. Alfano's final material still represents, roughly speaking, the last quarter of an hour of the opera.

> **Franco Alfano** (1875–1954), a Neapolitan, completed *Turandot*, rather like Süssmayer completed Mozart's *Requiem* after his death. Alfano composed several ballets and eleven operas, several of which were staged, including *L'ombra di Don Giovanni*, *Sakuntala*, and *Cyrano de Bergerac*. He spent much of his life teaching in various cities of Italy.

It is one of the tragedies of music that Puccini did not live to finish the love duet near the end of the opera, in which the two protagonists were to be transformed through love and which was to have been the focal point for the whole work. This was the love which, with the help of the orchestra, would suffuse everybody on the stage.

At the première,[1] Toscanini did not perform Alfano's conclusion. He

1 Various celebrities starred in the première: the Polish soprano Rosa Raisa, who Puccini himself had in mind for the title role; Miguel Fleta, the Spanish tenor, as the Unknown Prince Calaf; and Maria Zamboni as Liù.

stopped with the suicide of Liù. He turned to audience at this breathtaking moment and announced, 'Here Death triumphed over Art'. The audience left in silence.

In an infinitely less exalted way, the première featured a stand-off with Mussolini, the Italian dictator, who was in Milan for a political gathering. The La Scala management felt obliged to invite him. He refused to accept unless Toscanini performed the Fascist anthem at the start of the evening. Toscanani, who had had a brush with Mussolini about playing that anthem a couple of years before, refused to do this, so Mussolini refused to attend.

Turandot has been called the consummation of Puccini's creative career, blending elements such as the lyric-sentimental Liù, the heroic grandiose Turandot and Calaf, and the comic grotesque Venetian 'Masks', the court officials Ping, Pang and Pong. None of his other operas achieve this synthesis. But in doing so, *Turandot* is very different, and unique.

Carlo Gozzi (1722–1806) was a downwardly mobile Venetian nobleman, playwright, wit and satirist, and a contemporary of the lawyer Carlo Goldoni (who once wrote sixteen comedies in a year, and was the writer of many libretti).

Gozzi was a leading light in a group of literary wits who called themselves the 'Testicular Society'. The group's symbol was an owl and two testicles, and it chose as its president – the arch-testicle – an unfortunate dwarf who had pretensions to be a poet.

Gozzi and his friends were fiercely opposed to the new realistic style of writing introduced by Goldoni. To differentiate himself from his rival, Gozzi wrote fables, including *Re Turandote* and *The Love for Three Oranges* on which Prokofiev based his opera.

Gozzi's use of fairytales to convey his messages, including his misogyny, to a large audience was novel. Fairytales fascinate adults as much as children. Schiller observed that there was deeper meaning in the fairytales told to him in his childhood than in the truth that was taught by life.

At first, Gozzi was a tremendous success. Although Goldoni was driven away to France in 1762, where he remained until his death thirty years later, he finally won the day: Goldoni is today regarded as one of Italy's greatest playwrights.

WHO'S WHO AND WHAT'S WHAT

This summary is based on the libretto. As mentioned in the Warning at the end of this book, certain directors may amend opera stories to suit their production.

The opera is set in legendary times in Peking (Beijing) where the walls are festooned with the severed heads of suitors who have failed to win the hand of **Princess Turandot**, the daughter of the ancient **Chinese Emperor** Altoum. The only man she will marry is a Prince who can solve **three riddles**. Any suitor who fails to do so will die.

The opera opens with a **Mandarin** announcing the latest casualty. Among the bloodthirsty crowd watching the spectacle, there is a slave girl **Liù**, the carer of an old man who falls in the crush and chaos. Also there is a fugitive, an **Unknown Prince**, who recognises that the old man is his father **Timur**, the deposed Emperor. In earlier, better, times, the Unknown Prince had smiled at Liù.

The latest suitor, the **Prince of Persia**, goes to the block after Turandot, who does not sing at all in the first act, gives the thumbs down. When the Unknown Prince sees her, he is overcome with her beauty. He wants to risk his head and enter the contest.

Three comical court officials, **Ping** (the Grand Chancellor), **Pang** (the Purveyor General) and **Pong** (the Chief Cook), try to dissuade him, as does Liù. But he strikes the **gong** to signify his suit.

Ping, Pang and Pong, called collectively **the Masks**, long for this sorry business to come to an end. They go to the next ceremony of riddles predicting the inevitable outcome.

People congregate in front of the Imperial Palace during an orchestral interlude. The Emperor himself tries unsuccessfully to persuade the Unknown Prince to withdraw. The Mandarin announces the rules. Turandot appears (and sings for the first time after an hour of opera) and explains that she is the reincarnation of an ancestor who was raped and killed years ago by the Tartars.[2] The bloodletting is her revenge for that.

The Unknown Prince answers correctly the first and second riddles,

2 The name 'Tartar' was applied to the Mongols who most cruelly ravaged and terrorised Asia and Europe in the thirteenth century AD. 'Tartarus' was the name by which the abyss of torment, beneath Hades, was called in classical mythology. The Mongols 'took no prisoners'. That the fictional Calaf is portrayed as a fugitive is intentionally ironic, as is Timur, the name of his absurdly weak father. That was also the name of Tamerlane, a ferocious and successful Mongol Emperor.

'Hope', and 'Blood'. When he also answers correctly the third, 'Turandot', she is distraught. Her father insists she abide by the rules, but she asks the Unknown Prince whether he will take her by force. He nobly suggests that if, before dawn, she can state his name, he too will forfeit his life.

Overnight, she takes drastic action to discover his name. In the garden of the palace, **heralds** threaten torture and death if the Unknown Prince's name is not revealed before dawn. An offstage choir and the Unknown Prince echo the cry 'Nobody shall sleep', *Nessun dorma!*

Ping, Pang and Pong offer the Unknown Prince comely women and jewels if he will leave. Aware of their own fraught position, they offer to flee with him.

Unfortunately, the Prince's father and Liù were seen with the Prince, and presumably know his name. To prevent the old man being tortured, Liù declares the she alone knows it, but will not disclose it. Why? Turandot asks her. True love, she replies, which Turandot will eventually discover.

At the sight of the **executioner** Pu-Tin-Pao and his assistants, who have come to torture her, Liù plunges a dagger into her heart.

Alone with Turandot, who still resists him, the Unknown Prince grabs her and kisses her passionately. The kiss transforms her into a loving woman.[3] At dawn, Turandot is still reluctant but he claims her. He gives her the answer: he is **Calaf**, the son of Timur, King of the Tartars. At the ceremony, Turandot tells her father she knows the Prince's name: it is Love. They embrace passionately.[4]

---

3 Birgit Nilsson, the soprano, described how Domingo's kiss in Verona was so long that the audience began to shout *Basta, basta, adesso* – 'Hey, that'll do, thank you'. Unfortunately, in the process, he infected her with tonsillitis which nearly put her out of subsequent performances.

4 In a Rome production, Calaf was on one side of a little Chinese bridge, and Turandot on the other. When she sings her final words, *Il suo nome è Amor*, Calaf was to charge over the bridge and embrace her. He forgot the bridge, tripped and fell into the stream.

TALKING POINTS

Giacomo Puccini (1858–1924)
Please see the summary of the life of Puccini on pages 159 and 160.

Puccini's Place as a Composer – a View
The view expressed on pages 161-163 is very relevant.

'Dot' or 'doh'?
There is compelling evidence that Puccini pronounced the final syllable of Turandot as 'doh' rather than 'dot'. Rosa Raisa, the first Turandot, was emphatic that the 't' was not pronounced. Dame Eva Turner, herself a great Turandot, who attended the première and who sang the part shortly thereafter, pronounced it without the 't'. And the 't' was not pronounced in the early recordings. In particular, the recording conducted by Tullio Serafin, who knew both Puccini and Toscanini, does not sound it. Besides, in certain of the Prince's passages, it is extraordinarily difficult to sing the 't' effectively, especially in some of the high registers. Also, enunciating the 't' can spoil the flow of the music in places.

The 't' seems to have crept in around 1960, with the recordings made then and The Metropolitan Opera production at that time. Perhaps the sounding of the 't' has something to do with Gozzi's play being named (in French) *Turandotte*, or with the German pronunciation of final consonants. Those who choose the silent 't' are certainly not wrong and are in good company, including that of the composer, even if today they may sound rather old-fashioned.

The 1990 football World Cup
Nessun dorma! ('Nobody shall sleep'), the 'best tune' in the opera, as sung by Luciano Pavarotti, and subsequently associated with him, was the theme song for the 1990 World Cup held in Italy. The recording reached number 2 in the UK singles chart, the highest rating achieved by a classical recording. It has been the largest-selling classical recording ever, and demonstrates the enduring power of *pre-modern* classical music: this aria from the 1920s was welcomed globally as suitable to complement this most popular sport.

The first 'Three Tenors' concert, featuring Luciano Pavarotti, Placido Domingo and José Carreras, under the baton of Zubin Mehta, was on 7 July, 1990. It was a celebrity occasion, held at the Baths of Caracalla, the outdoor opera venue in Rome, to celebrate the World Cup and Carreras's recovery from leukemia. The singers were all football fans. The three stars performed for a flat fee, albeit not modest, which Pavarotti said 'was not the smartest business deal any of them ever made'. Afterwards, as his agent put it, 'they didn't suffer in silence. The racket they made about it could be heard from Rome to California'.

When the concert was repeated in 1994 before the World Cup in Los Angeles, the terms were more lucrative. And then the Three Tenors went around the world, and kept going until the concept ran out of steam.

In this aria, the Unknown Prince Calaf, echoes the heralds who have proclaimed Turandot's edict that nobody shall sleep: unless his name is revealed by dawn, the city shall be put to the sword. He asserts that, at sunrise, he will win Turandot with a kiss: *All'alba vincerò*. It is presumably the *vincerò* – the 'winning' – rather than the kiss, which is more relevant to sport.

The affaire Doria

Puccini had a mistress, Elvira, for around twenty years, who he married after the death of her husband, in 1904. But he was bored with her: she had not kept pace with his success, and he was anyway a considerable womaniser. She was desperately jealous.

Elvira found him late at night chatting to the 21-year-old Doria Manfredi, one of the domestic servants at his house in Torre del Lago, near Lucca. Elvira became hysterical and started following Doria around the village, shrieking abuse. Doria was driven to commit an agonising suicide by drinking poison.

After this, the Manfredi family prosecuted Elvira, who was convicted, fined and sentenced to several months' imprisonment. The case was settled, so Elvira did not have to go to jail, but not surprisingly the whole matter caused Puccini enormous worry. Perhaps there is something of Elvira in the character of Turandot, and of Doria in the role of Liù.

Liù is entirely a creation of Puccini. Her music is far more pleasing to the ear than Turandot's: for example, in *Signore ascolta*, she ends high on a gentle B flat, but does not shriek. She is the only main character in the story who actually 'touches the heart.'

However, not only is Liù redundant to the drama, she also creates a dramatic problem. Her death is so final and so shocking that it provides a false close to the opera. It was where Puccini broke off before he died. It is particularly unfortunate that he was not alive to finalise the subsequent final scene. It would have been interesting to see how he would have revived the drama and tension after such an apparently complete ending.

Turandot – her music

The part of Turandot is static and extremely difficult – even 'unsingable' – although fortunately it is short. Until the end of the opera there is little trace of lyricism. It can only be performed by powerful, imposing sopranos capable of singing 'throat-wrenching high tones', such as Birgit Nilsson (1918–2005). After the kiss, Turandot's 'tones like sharpened steel' at last transmute into 'warm sounds of love and pity'.

In her *In questa Reggia* in which she explains her actions, Turandot sings at the top of the soprano range. There are various moments when she sustains a high C.[5] Perhaps the most dramatic is in act 2, when, having sworn that never shall man possess her, Turandot reaches what has been described as 'probably the most dreaded high C of all'. She shrieks *Gli enigma sono tre, la morte è una* ('the riddles are three, death is but one'). At the same time, the man, in unison, reaching the top C of his tenor range, cries out *Gli enigma sono tre, una è la vita* ('the riddles are three, life is but one').[6]

They also reach high C, albeit separately, at the dramatic moment at the end of act 2 when the Prince has solved the riddles and she protests, 'Will you take me in your arms forcibly?' and he replies, 'No, I want you ablaze with love'.[7]

The sustained high C can be an athletic achievement rather than an artistic one. Birgit Nilsson recalled that Franco Corelli 'could apparently sustain this tone for ever'. According to her, he had 'one of the most fantastic tenor voices ever'. But whether his sustained high C fitted with 'any style, or was in good taste, is another matter'. That question can usually be repeated today.

Turandot – the character

Turandot, 'the pathologically icy princess', the 'neurotic murderer' is a detestable woman, an 'inhuman monster'. Her cruelty and barbarism dominate the opera. Puccini deliberately exaggerated the ghastliness of Gozzi's

---

5 In Mozart's *The Magic Flute*, the Queen of the Night reaches D and F above high C. But that is sung as part of a coloratura run, and the notes are not sustained. The greatest sopranos such as Maria Callas and Joan Sutherland have found the E flats in the Mad Scene in *Lucia di Lammermoor* have provided a challenge.

6 Nilsson suggested that 'there is probably no tenor who can dynamically overpower the high C of a soprano in his natural voice'. She described how one well-known tenor just spread his arms and opened his mouth wide and everybody thought that both he and the soprano had sung high C. She also infers that one great tenor ensured that he ducked behind Turandot for this purpose.

7 For this, Puccini also provides the Prince with a less demanding alternative.

Turandot.[8] For example, Puccini's answers to the three riddles are 'Hope', 'Blood' and 'Turandot'; whereas for Gozzi they were 'The sun', 'The year' and 'The Venetian lion'. Indeed, it might seem that the appearance of Turandot in act 1 in a non-singing role was a deliberate attempt by the composer to avoid her character being compatible with the beauty of music.

We are told by enthusiasts that 'Puccini desired with all his heart and mind to glorify Love'. But he seems to have confused sex with love, a magazine image with a person. Nobody could possibly love this vengeful heroine, this 'flint-hearted beauty'.

Thus Calaf, far from displaying nobility and generosity, can appear to be a fool. He is a fool for falling for Turandot in the first place; then, having not lost his head literally, he loses it figuratively by releasing her from her side of the bargain. He takes yet a further risk by disclosing his name to her before dawn. Gozzi tells us, however, that 'the brightest intellect is no defence when love assails'. That seems clear in this case.

The Prince at times almost seems (unintentionally) comical. When Turandot claims that she is the daughter of Heaven, and her soul is on high, his response is hilarious: *la tua anima è in alto, ma il tuo corpo è vicino* ('Your soul may be on high but your body is down here'). He grabs her and kisses her passionately. This is the climax of the opera. It is reminiscent of the moment in Verdi's *Il Trovatore* when Leonora, about to become a nun, asks to be led to the altar. The bully-boy Count, her would-be lover, exclaims: 'the only altar for you, lady, is the nuptial altar'.

Commedia dell'arte and chinoiserie
Ping, Pang and Pong are redolent of the *Commedia dell'arte* clowns, such as Harlequin and Pantaloon, which were a feature of the traditional strolling masked players who improvised their ribald humour, often featuring sex, disease, cuckolds and geriatrics. These 'Venetian Masks' were also modelled in Meissen 'Chinese' porcelain, and are predecessors to some of the characters in Mozart's *The Magic Flute*.[9]

They were central to the dispute between Gozzi and his contemporary Goldoni. Gozzi wanted to retain them as part of the historical legacy

---

8 Liù's equivalent in Gozzi's tale is Adelma, a conquered princess, now the slave of Turandot, and a rival to her mistress for the love of Calaf. Turandot's love-hate conflict makes her a far more complex character than in the opera. She is 'an eighteenth-century spokeswoman for modern woman's liberation', although she concludes the play by declaring that men are perhaps not so bad after all. The play contains the possibility of a lesbian relationship between the two princesses.
9 Mozart's Papageno is derived from Gozzi's clown Truffaldino.

of Italian theatre, and he included them in his fairytales. Goldoni, the revisionist and modernist, thought these crude low-brow stereotypes had passed their 'sell-by date' and excluded them from his dramas.

Having chosen a fable by Gozzi as the basis of his libretto, Puccini was faced with how to incorporate these characters. Although at times Puccini and his librettists thought of eliminating them, in the end he adopted them fully. His sinister and sadistic Masks play a direct role and provide much Shakespearian light relief as a contrast to the awfulness of the drama, whereas in Gozzi's play they just stand by as chorus. Puccini gave them some delightful music, for example when Ping wishes that they could get away to their country homes, in *Ho una casa nell'Honan*.

From the outset the orchestra provides a 'Chinese' sound. The percussion is augmented with a variety of drums, cymbals, triangles, xylophones, and bells and gongs of various sizes. Some of the tunes, including the final melodies, are actual Chinese tunes which Puccini possibly took from an old Chinese musical box belonging to a friend. He drew on Chinese folk songs for two of the themes associated with the Masks.

The outcome is, for European ears, highly exotic. Only time will tell whether Chinese people find this chinoiserie, not least the comic Ping, Pang and Pong, acceptable and politically correct.

Hardly lovable: the great Eva Turner

ACT BY ACT

Act 1 The walls of Peking
The orchestra opens with a menacing four-bar fortissimo which leaves us in no doubt of the drama to come and the unpleasant character of Turandot. There is considerable bitonal dissonance, with various instruments playing in two different keys. The xylophone informs us that we are in the Far East.

We are at the walls of Peking (Beijing) in legendary times. They are festooned by spikes with severed heads on them. A Mandarin announces the edict that Princess Turandot will marry a Prince who solves three riddles that she has set. But he who tries and fails will be beheaded. At the rising of the moon, the most recent suitor, the Prince of Persia, is due to meet his fate.

The bloodthirsty mob[10] is so enthusiastic that it has to be repelled by the soldiers. In the mêlée, an Unknown Prince comes to the assistance of an old man and his carer, the slave girl Liù. The Unknown Prince recognises the old man as his father Timur, once the Emperor, who was defeated, deposed and like him became a fugitive. Liù volunteered to accompany him because one day in the palace the Prince smiled at her: *Perchè un dì ... mi hai sorriso.*

To the encouragement of the mob, the executioner and his assistants oil and sharpen the sword with which the head of the Prince of Persia will be struck off. The mob eagerly awaits the rising of the moon, when the execution will take place: *Perchè tarda la luna?* It looks forward to a succession of suitors who will strike the gong to enter the contest. (To Placido Domingo, the chorus to the moon, when as a young performer he first heard it, was 'one of the most moving experiences of his life'.)

The moon rises and the march to the scaffold begins. At the sight of the wretched Prince of Persia, the mood of the crowd changes from bloodlust to pity. High on the battlements, Turandot appears, lit by the moon, *come una visione* – like an apparition – and, with a blast on the brass, gives the Persian Prince the Peking equivalent of a 'thumbs-down'. But she does not utter.

The Unknown Prince is overcome with the sight and beauty of Turandot, despite the protestations of his father and Liù. A distant last cry 'Turandot' from the victim on the scaffold can be heard. The Unknown Prince rushes to the gong, which he must strike three times if he wants to claim her.

---

10 Puccini's use of the chorus throughout the opera is masterly.

Before the Prince can strike the gong, three imperial civil servants or courtiers intervene: Ping, Pang and Pong.[11] They are respectively Grand Chancellor, Purveyor General and Chief Cook. Although rather more concerned about their own survival than the Prince's, they urge him to leave: why waste a good life on one woman? If she is stripped naked, she is just flesh. There are many alternatives, in the form of Turandot's comely ladies-in-waiting, who now attempt to seduce him. And he is reminded of his fate by the spirits of former participants in the contest.

The executioner reappears and places the head of the Prince of Persia on a spike. In a complete contrast, Liù desperately (but the melody is beautiful, as is the orchestration with harp, woodwind and muted violins) makes a final attempt to plead with the Prince – *Signore ascolta* ('Listen, Lord, listen') – but with no success: *Non piangere, Liù!* He asks her to look after his father, if he fails.

The stately climax builds as Ping, Pang and Pong again try to dissuade him, assisted by the spirits of former participants. To no avail. But the Unknown Prince strikes the gong three times, and the orchestra in a sudden and dramatic change of key blasts out the theme associated with Turandot. The crowd reckon they might as well start digging his grave.

Act 2 In a Chinese pavilion, then the palace square

This is a contrast to the previous scene. The first scene in the act is devoted to Ping, Pang and Pong. And the detail in the score from the outset is considerable, especially in the percussion department. The three 'Masks' move from the serious to the comic, falsetto to natural, loud to soft and so on.

In a Chinese pavilion, Ping, Pang and Pong, having heard the gong, know that their job is to prepare either for a wedding or for a funeral. They look through the records and recall the executions. In the current Year of the Tiger, this suitor will be the thirteenth. In a change to a nostalgic mood, they wish they could get back to their country houses rather than have to organise all this: *Ho una casa nell'Honan*, which at first is principally accompanied by the celesta 'più piano possibile'. They recall the fate of the Prince of Samarkand, the Indian, the Burmese and the Prince of Kirghiz. In a change of mood, they long for the nuptials of the royal lovers. They optimistically hope that they will serenade the Princess of China, who has become intoxicated by love, having previously been ice-cold and despising it: *Non v'è in Cina.*

They hear the sound of the palace awakening, and Ping brings them back to reality. They hurry off to the next ceremony of riddles.

---

11 Their intervention is sung to a snippet from the imperial Chinese national anthem.

During a beautiful orchestral interlude with the full orchestra, a colossal sound, the dignitaries congregate in the square in front of the Imperial Palace, and the crowd wishes that the Emperor may live 10,000 years. The already ancient Emperor is on his throne at the top of a stairway; sages hold scrolls with the solutions to the three riddles. There is a great fanfare.

The monarch, so decrepit he can hardly utter, then unsuccessfully beseeches the virile Unknown Prince to withdraw: there has been enough blood. The Mandarin again proclaims the law that Princess Turandot will marry whoever of royal blood will solve the three riddles. He who tries and fails will be beheaded: *Popolo di Pekino*. From behind the scenes, boys sing a tune which Puccini seems to have heard on an old Chinese musical box belonging to a friend.

Turandot appears for the ceremony. At last, she sings. Her voice rages higher and higher as she recalls how thousands of years ago her ancestor had been raped and killed by the Tartars: *In questa Reggia*. This ancestor is reincarnated in her; she now avenges her ancestor's scream and death. She, Turandot, will never be possessed by man. After several Bs, her voice climaxes with a pause on top C as she threatens that the riddles are three, death is one. The Unknown Prince declares 'No, life is one!'. The crowd presses for the ceremony to begin.

The ceremony is orchestrated to the thinnest of orchestration: the tension is in the drama, and the orchestra does not distract from it. Turandot reads the first of the three riddles. The Prince's answer, 'Hope', is confirmed by the sages. The Prince slowly reaches the right answer to the second: 'Blood'. Like a bird about to seize its prey, Turandot screeches the third into the Unknown Prince's face: ice which gives him fire ... he has difficulty working it out, but, to Turandot's horror, he finds the answer: 'Turandot'. This is confirmed by the sages. To the Chinese theme, the crowd hails him the victor.

Distraught, Turandot then argues with her father whether she has to submit: *Figlio del cielo; padre augusto!* She swears that no man shall possess her. Her father will not release her from her original vow, and the crowd is against her, so she asks the Prince (hitting high C) whether he wants to take her by force, a reluctant frigid bride. No, he replies, he wants her ablaze with love.

There is a complete pause, of almost a bar. He nobly releases her from her side of the bargain. She gave him three riddles to solve, but he will put to her but one: he challenges her to state his name.[12] If she finds

---

12 We begin to hear, at first in the strings and then the woodwind, the love theme, later the basis of *Nessun dorma*.

it out before dawn, he will forfeit his life: *Tre enigmi m'hai proposto!* The Emperor hopes he becomes his son-in-law. The crowd applauds the Emperor.

Act 3 The palace garden, then outside

It is night-time in the garden of the palace, conveyed with beautifully, almost perfumed, orchestration, with harp glissandos. The Unknown Prince hears eight heralds announcing Turandot's command: nobody may sleep; the stranger's name must be disclosed before morning, or the populace will be put to the sword. The desperate people, offstage, echo *come un lamento*. In the famous aria, which is so deliberately such a total contrast to the cold icy sounds we have heard before, the Prince also echoes their cry 'Nobody shall sleep', *Nessun dorma!* Yes, his name is his secret. But, her ice-cold frigidity will melt when he reveals it to her with a kiss. At dawn, he will be a conqueror: *All'alba vincerò!*

Meanwhile, Ping, Pang and Pong, desperate, greatly afraid for their own future, parade comely, veiled, odalisques before the Prince. We hear that the maidens would look even more attractive with fewer clothes on them.[13] The civil servants also offer him jewels, also unsuccessfully; and, contemplating their own fraught position, they offer to flee with him. They remind him of her cruelty if he does not reveal his name; they threaten him. But the increasingly desperate Prince is adamant that all he wants is Turandot: *Crollasse il mondo, voglio Turandot*, even if the world falls apart, he wants Turandot.

There is an interruption when the Prince's father Timur, and Liù, are dragged in. Ping saw them with the Prince, and they presumably know the secret of his name. They are threatened by the mob if they do not immediately disclose it. The civil servants rush to fetch Turandot, who reappears, taunts the Prince, and orders Timur to disclose the name.

The Prince's father remains silent. Before he can be tortured, Liù declares that she alone knows the name but she will not disclose it – she would rather die. Despite the crowd's baying for blood and guts, despite the threat of torture, which is implemented, she will not reveal it. Turandot, in amazement, wonders what has steeled her heart with so much strength. Love, true love, she declares, accompanied by a solo violin: *Principessa, l'amore, tanto amore*. Indeed, so much love, secret and undisclosed, that the torture is sweetness for her. Liù bequeaths the Prince to her, and thereby loses any hope she herself ever had.

---

13 The surging orchestra depicts their voluptuous figures. Their 'tabloid-newspaper-page-3' aspects are characterised by their conversation being limited to a repetition of the single word 'Ah'. Puccini has a marvellous sense of humour.

When the mighty executioner is called in to exert more pressure, Liù fears she will not have the strength to resist. She foretells that, despite Turandot's icy frigidity, *Tu che di gel sei cinta*, she too will eventually come to love him. The crowd calls for her to reveal the name. She manages to rush through the crowd, grab a dagger from a soldier and plunge it into her heart. As she falls at the feet of Prince, he and his father are distraught. Turandot seizes a whip and strikes the soldier in the face.

Ping tells the father that she is dead: he might as well get up. The old man warns that Liù's spirit will take revenge. The victim of injustice will become a vampire. In what has been described as 'one of the most moving scenes in all opera', the crowd's attitude changes. With the basses descending to E, (F flat), the crowd prays for forgiveness. The dead Liù is taken away, the old man holding her hand, going, as he knows, to die of grief. (This was the point which Puccini reached before he died; the rest of the opera was completed by Alfano.)

Everyone disperses, apart from the Prince and Turandot, who haughtily still resists him. The Prince rips her veil away. 'Keep back,' she protests. She is the daughter of Heaven, and her soul is on high. The Prince responds, *la tua anima è in alto, ma il tuo corpo è vicino* ('Your soul may be on high but your body is here!'). He grabs her and kisses her passionately. She yields. The kiss transforms her from the ice-cold princess into a loving woman.

Voices behind the scene hail the rising dawn. In an aria that provides a considerable contrast to her act 2 narration, Turandot admits to the Prince that, when she first saw him, she knew he was special, and feared she would love him: *Del primo pianto*. But she still tries to resist him. Surely, he has achieved his objective with the kiss. 'Go no further: go away and carry your mystery (your name) with you.' 'There's no mystery any more,' shouts the Prince, 'You're mine!' He gives her his name, Calaf, the son of Timur, and thereby places his life in her hands. They leave for the ceremonial questioning of his name.

Outside the palace, Turandot, conquered at last, tells her father she knows the Prince's name: it is Love (on B flat). The couple embrace passionately, to the applause of the crowd (to the tune of *Nessun dorma*).

Puccini's Other Operas
Le Villi
Edgar
La Rondine

The young Puccini

Contents

Le Villi: Background

When he was nearly twenty-two, Puccini began three years of study at the Milan Conservatoire. He was financed by a scholarship and also by a great-uncle, a bachelor, who was a well-known doctor in his home town of Lucca. His diploma qualified him to be called a 'Maestro', a term perhaps then more widely used than today when it tends to be reserved as a mark of respect for a distinguished conductor.

He wanted to become an opera composer. *Le Villi* was his first opera. One of his teachers at the Conservatoire, Amilcare Ponchielli (1834–1886), the composer of *La Gioconda* (1876), was particularly supportive. He encouraged the young man to enter for the 'Concorso Sonzogno', a new competition for one-act operas. A few years later, Puccini's fellow student Mascagni would win this prize with his *Cavalleria rusticana*.

Ponchielli also introduced him to Giulio Ricordi, the influential publisher, and to Ferdinando Fontana, a writer and radical journalist who would write the libretto for his entry. To his cost, Puccini later discovered Fontana's limitations as a dramatic librettist.

Fontana's libretto was based on a tale from European folklore used for *Giselle, ou Les Wilis*, the very successful French ballet about[1] the ghosts of girls who died of grief after being abandoned by their lovers. These 'witch-dancers' would take revenge by dancing the men to death.

Fontana was not an easy character to deal with. He was almost nine years older than Puccini and had already written several libretti, quantity rather than quality. Once Fontana's fee was settled – not a straightforward matter – Puccini began work. He just managed to enter his opera by the competition deadline. But his score was so illegible that possibly the judges did not, or could not, give it serious consideration. His name did not even get a mention.

Fortunately Fontana was as keen as Puccini to see the work staged, and with Ponchielli's help, Puccini was invited to play at the Milan salon of a prominent and wealthy supporter of the arts.

Present that evening was Arrigo Boito, best known today for being Verdi's librettist for both *Otello* and *Falstaff*, and also Ponchielli's librettist for *La Gioconda*. At the time, Boito was recognised as 'the foremost arbiter of Milan's intellectual and artistic taste'. The evening went so well

---

1 The music of *Giselle* was by Adolphe Adam, the French composer. It was first performed in 1841 in Paris. Puccini first called his opera *Le Willis*, but later Italianised it to *Le Villi*.

that the gathering decided to raise the finance to get *Le Villi* staged.

On 31 May, 1884, *Le Villi* was 'a sensational success' at its première in the Teatro dal Verme, one of Milan's leading theatres.[2] Was Puccini the composer for whom Italy had been waiting? He was compared with Bizet and Massenet. His melody and his symphonic writing for the orchestra were praised. He showed a feel for the theatre and for characterisation. His opera even received a compliment from the elderly Verdi, who rarely praised the work of the younger generation.

Puccini followed Ricordi's advice and made substantial revisions and additions, including restructuring the one-act opera into two acts. This version was very successful in Turin. Subsequently, critics at La Scala and at the San Carlo in Naples disliked the prominent part given to the orchestra, which they thought showed unfortunate 'Wagnerian' tendencies. But *Le Villi* went on to be performed widely abroad.

Listening to *Le Villi*, to its melodies and fine orchestral sequences, it is not difficult to imagine the excitement among those attending that Milan salon evening when Puccini played the score. His opera may lack drama, tension and interplay between the characters, but the music is most enjoyable.

The success of *Le Villi* enabled Ricordi to present Puccini with the first one-thousand lire note that he had ever held. Ricordi also commissioned Puccini to compose a full-length opera to be performed at La Scala. Was his previous Bohemian existence a thing of the past? It must have seemed as if he had made a breakthrough. But the dawn was false.

Unfortunately, Fontana was specified as the librettist of his next opera, *Edgar*, which was a fiasco.

---

2 Mascagni played the double bass in the orchestra.

Who's Who and What's What:

Le Villi

This summary is based on the libretto. As mentioned in the Warning at the end of this book, certain directors may amend opera stories to suit their production.

In spring-time in the Black Forest, in South Germany, the betrothal of **Anna** and **Roberto** is being celebrated. He is about to leave for Mainz on the River Rhine to collect a fortune which he has unexpectedly inherited. Anna is apprehensive; but Roberto professes his undying love for her. Her father **Guglielmo** blesses them.

The outcome is told by a **Narrator**,[3] while the orchestra plays the first part of the **intermezzo**: in Mainz, a whore lured Roberto into the fleshpots; he abandoned and forgot Anna, who died of grief waiting for him. To the music of The Witches' Sabbath, the Narrator then describes the 'Willis', who await men who have abandoned their lover. They surround the man and dance him to death.

In act 2, Guglielmo bewails the loss of his daughter; he hopes that the Willis will take revenge. Roberto, remorseful and penniless, returns. But it is too late. The night is fearsome with strange sounds, so different from those happy days in May, when love bloomed. He hears Anna's voice reproaching him. She draws him towards her. The Willis dance around him, spinning and turning. Anna will not let him escape, but forces him to join the frenzied dance. He falls dead of exhaustion at her feet. 'You are mine!' she declares.

---

3 Possibly it was originally intended that these verses should merely be read by the audience. Fontana believed that an printed opera synopsis should be a work of art in its own right.

TALKING POINTS: LE VILLI

Giacomo Puccini (1858–1924)
Please see the summary of the life of Puccini on pages 159 and 160.

Puccini's Place as a Composer – a View
The view expressed on pages 161-163 is very relevant.

EDGAR: BACKGROUND

For the next opera, Fontana, the librettist of *Le Villi*, supplied Puccini with a 'baffling', 'preposterous' libretto for a grand opera. It was based on a lengthy verse-play written half a century earlier by the distinguished French poet Alfred de Musset. It was adapted from his 'La Coupe et les Lèvres' (Between Cup and Lip). This was a mystical and spiritual play, to be read rather than to be staged. Little of Musset's perplexing original survived in the opera.

Puccini had no choice: the librettist had been nominated. He was in an impossible position. He struggled with an indigestible libretto which posed a virtually insuperable challenge. Any sense of drama is eclipsed by its complexity.

Maybe Fontana envisaged creating a second *Carmen*. Just as in Bizet's opera the Spanish gypsy seduces Don José away from the chaste Micaëla, so Tigrana, a Moorish 'she-devil', tempts Edgar from his bride Fidelia. There is a more muscular male in the background, the soldier of fortune Frank, even though he seems more like a captain of a school cadet force than a toreador. Fidelia is stabbed by Tigrana, who is then lynched off-stage as the curtain falls.

The aptly named Fidelia represents pure love; Tigrana, sung by a mezzo-soprano, represents a shameful form of love, *un amore abietto, indegno*. To a modern audience, this distinction may seem somewhat simplistic, even artificial, and the moral implications unstimulating. One would suspect that the composer himself faced a similar difficulty, even embarrassment: he was cuckolding a school-friend at the time.

At the end of the opera, Edgar claims to have received the means of 'redemption',[4] a blessing not accorded to Bizet's unfortunate Don José. This highfalutin notion was difficult to handle successfully: 'southern audiences do not generally care for the representation of moral themes on the operatic stage'.

It would be five years before *Edgar* was performed, in Milan in 1889. Not only did Puccini have to contend with the libretto, but his work was interrupted by the death of his mother and by the practical consequences of the affair with his singing pupil. Elvira saddled him with two step-children and gave him a third. And his great-uncle, whose crucial financial support had terminated with the award of his diploma, wanted his cash back: if the young man could afford a mistress, he was also able to repay a loan.

---

4 Such as is found in Wagner's opera *Tannhäuser*.

Also, Puccini was a slow worker. While time marched on, Giulio Ricordi, his publisher – see pages 12 & 13 – increasingly impatient but still supportive, kept him afloat with a monthly advance.

The première of *Edgar* was on 21 April, 1889. For the title role, Puccini tried to attract Francesco Tamagno, a friend from his time at the Milan Conservatoire. But this tenor who, a couple of years before had created Verdi's Otello, was away abroad. For the part of Tigrana, which at that stage was a far bigger role and had four great soprano arias to sing, he engaged Romilda Pantaleoni: she had created Desdemona, but her abilities and enthusiasm for the role were questionable. The conductor was her lover, Franco Faccio.

Edgar was a failure: it was coolly received; only three performances were given. Ricordi wanted it to be rescued. But Fontana, who seems to have been incredibly stubborn, resisted changes. Puccini cut it down to three acts, changed Tigrana's part from soprano to mezzo-soprano, and later revised it yet again. Thereby, it became an 'unexplained succession of bizarre situations'. Unfortunately, his frequently very fine and enjoyable music cannot compensate for the opera's incomprehensibility and dramatic weaknesses.

Puccini knew that the opera was dramatically hopeless: it was far too complicated for an audience to grasp. Some of his revisions[5] were extraordinary and suggest that he was (understandably) utterly fed up and could not be bothered with it. He created a duet, *Ah Edgar, dal labbro mio*, in act 2 in which seductive music originally designed for Fidelia was given to Tigrana to sing. This made an unforgivable nonsense of two entirely distinct roles.

A production in Madrid failed to fire despite its star cast.

Ricordi had some difficulty in persuading his fellow-directors that his business should continue to support Puccini financially. He reverted to living in straitened circumstances. However, on 1 February, 1893, his aspirations were at last rewarded, and Ricordi's support justified, with the success of *Manon Lescaut*.

Puccini correctly regarded *Edgar* as a 'blunder'.[6] At best, it must be regarded as a kind of educational exercise, a rite of passage. It enabled him to develop his skill at large choruses. But the venture carried major risks, particularly financial: it condemned him to penury for several years. He contemplated emigrating to Argentina to join his brother as a music teacher. He would only once again, and then when off guard, make such a mistake again. That was over a quarter of a century later with *La Rondine*.

5 The definitive version is that performed in Buenos Aires in 1905.
6 In a score which he gave to his friend Sybil Seligman, he wrote: 'E Dio ti Gu A Rdi da quest' opera', 'God preserve you from this opera'.

WHO'S WHO AND WHAT'S WHAT:

EDGAR

This summary is based on the libretto. As mentioned in the Warning at the end of this book, certain directors may amend opera stories to suit their production.

In Flanders in 1302: **Edgar** is asleep in front of the tavern while the locals go to their work in the fields. **Fidelia** comes to greet him and then she rushes off.

Tigrana, a Moorish girl, abandoned as a baby fifteen years ago, appears. She has bewitched Fidelia's brother **Frank**. He is angry because she did not turn up to a date on the previous evening.

Edgar also fancies Tigrana, and throws up everything to leave with her for an orgy of passion, sex and money. He even burns his house.

Frank tries to stop them going. When a fight ensues, **Gualtiero**, the father of Frank and Fidelia, intervenes. But Edgar wounds Frank and leaves with Tigrana. Frank curses him.

***

In the garden of his castle, where an orgy is taking place, Edgar has tired of sensual pleasure. He longs for a change. Tigrana realises that he loves her no more. She tries to persuade him that there is no return to the past: they are inextricably joined together.

When a regiment of soldiers is heard passing by, Edgar instantly decides to join up. Its commander happens to be Frank. If Edgar enlists and fights by Frank's side, they can make it up between themselves. Despite Tigrana's protests, Edgar breaks away and goes off to fight.

***

A funeral is taking place; a Requiem is sung. Fidelia, utterly grief-stricken, and Gualtiero are in the cortège. Frank is accompanied by a **Monk** whose identity is disguised by the cowl which covers his face.

There has been a battle in which, so it seems, Edgar behaved heroically and was killed in the cause of freedom. Frank starts to deliver the oration.

The Monk (actually, Edgar himself) disputes Frank's eulogy, and draws attention to Edgar's considerable failings: he burnt his family home; he wounded Frank; and, with Tigrana he frequented fleshpots and gambling joints. He was just an ordinary soldier of fortune, and had everything to gain and nothing to lose by being brave. Besides, next to his castle, there was a wood in which people disappeared. Maybe he was a murderer.

The crowd, whose mood has turned hostile, is about to attack the catafalque. But Fidelia intervenes to stop them.

***

When the crowd disperses, Tigrana comes seemingly to grieve for Edgar. The Monk (Edgar) and Frank decide to test her sincerity. She is disturbed and reluctant. But with a display of dazzling jewels and appalling immorality, Edgar (the Monk) eventually succeeds in bribing her to accuse Edgar of treachery. In return for the jewels, she lies that Edgar intended to betray his country.

The outraged soldiers are about to throw his body to the crows, when they find that the armour is empty.

The Monk reveals himself as Edgar. Fidelia rushes to embrace him. He declares himself redeemed.[7] He curses Tigrana who stabs Fidelia. Edgar falls on her body, while Tigrana is lynched.

---

7 The grounds for this are not explained. By any normal ethical standards, the diabolical Edgar should go to hell!

TALKING POINTS: EDGAR

Giacomo Puccini (1858–1924)
Please see the summary of the life of Puccini on pages 159 and 160.

Puccini's Place as a Composer – a View
The view expressed on pages 161-163 is very relevant.

The context: the Battle of the Spurs
The setting of the opera is near Courtray (Kortrijk) in Flanders, in1302. The town, which was originally Roman, is located twenty-six miles south-west of Ghent in modern Belgium.

In 1302, the 'Battle of the Spurs' took place at Courtray. In this, twenty thousand Flemings, mainly weavers from Ghent and Bruges, destroyed a French army of twice the size, led by seven thousand knights and nobles. About seven hundred gilt spurs were collected on the battlefield and hung up as a trophy in a convent nearby.

LA RONDINE: BACKROUND

A century or more ago, those not actually shocked by the fallen woman, 'La Traviata', would be fascinated by her. She was a good subject commercially. This had been demonstrated by Marguerite in Alexandre Dumas's sensationally successful novel *La Dame aux Camélias*: she left her rich lover and fell for a fresh-faced youth up from the country. Puccini's courtesan in search of true love did much the same.

Marguerite, who became Verdi's Violetta, was punished for her sins by dying tragically of tuberculosis. However, Puccini's Magda, like the swallow, 'La Rondine', after her flight to the sun in search of true love, flew back to the nest from whence she came.[8]

La Rondine is rarely performed today. This comparison of different types of love was unsuitable as an opera: it was too complex for an audience to comprehend without distracting them from the music. And the production was caught up in the slipstream of the First World War.

In autumn 1913, Puccini went to Vienna for the production of his *La Fanciulla del West* at the Court opera. The commercially-minded management[9] of the Karltheater seized the opportunity to suggest that he might fancy writing eight or ten numbers which would fit into the spoken dialogue of one of the operettas in which their theatre specialised.[10] They offered him a phenomenally lucrative contract, with fifty-percent royalties. But he turned this down because he sensed that operetta was not his field.

After his baptism of fire with *Edgar*, Puccini's antennae were normally very acute indeed. But by Spring 1914, when he was again in Vienna, this time for the début of the Czech soprano Maria Jeritza as Tosca, his judgement had been blunted by years of success and by a recent row with Tito Ricordi (see page 13). His intransigent publisher had declined to keep to the usual routine and accompany his client to the event. Ricordi chose instead to attend an opera for which he himself had written the libretto. At the last minute, he also peremptorily withdrew the substitute he intended to send along, and he ignored Puccini's protestations.

Puccini took revenge: he signed a contract with the Karltheater directors. The operetta, which he envisaged as a reaction against what

---

8 'Rondine', swallow, is pronounced with the same emphasis as the English word 'holiday'.
9 Heinrich Berté, known for his sentimental and very successful musical on the life of Schubert entitled *Lilac Time*, and Otto Eibenschütz.
10 Prunier's romanza, Magda's aria, Lisette's duet with Prunier, and the waltzes, would appear to be such numbers.

he called 'the repulsive music of today', was to be in German, be based on a subject chosen by the directors, and be dramatised by a well-known Viennese librettist, Willner. Puccini rejected the first scenario with which he was presented a few months later. It was, he said, 'banal and clumsy, with no characterisation, originality or interest'.

Willner assisted by Reichert, another Viennese librettist, prepared an alternative, a cross between *La Traviata* (with a bit of humour thrown in) and Johann Strauss's *Die Fledermaus* (in which a saucy maid dressed up in her boss's fashionable clothing goes to a ball).

Puccini set to work with all his usual attention to detail and craftsmanship. Nevertheless, as he progressed, he developed an increasing dislike of the 'filth' (*porcheria*) as he called it. He began to curse the moment he had signed the contract in Vienna. He brought in his own librettist Giuseppe Adami[11] to prepare an Italian version. He replaced the dialogue with lyrics which enabled him to 'spread himself' in the music. What had started as an operetta evolved into a full-length opera.

Adami, after much rewriting, and after complying with Puccini's infuriating demands, produced a version which was acceptable.[12] *La Rondine* was completed to Puccini's satisfaction by Easter 1916.

On 14 May, 1915, Italy, having been neutral at the start of World War I, declared war on Austro-Hungary. The première could no longer be held in Vienna. Besides, communication with the enemy was impossible. Puccini tried to interest Ricordi in publishing *La Rondine*, but without success: Ricordi just dismissed it as 'bad Léhar'.[13] Sonzogno, Ricordi's rival, published it, and did a deal with the Viennese.

When the première of *La Rondine* was scheduled, one French journalist accused those involved of 'culpable commerce with the enemy'. Puccini protested that he had taken property away from the enemy and given it to an Italian publisher.

The première, on 27 March, 1917, was held in Monte Carlo. Two distinguished singers Tito Schipa and Gilda dalla Rizza, were in the lead roles. The critics wrote of its 'rich inspiration' and 'freshness'. But, arguably it is precisely these qualities that it lacks. The fact that it is neither opera nor operetta sealed its fate.

---

11 Giuseppe Adami (1878–1946) was the librettist of *La Rondine* and *Turandot* and a biographer of Puccini.
12 Willner and Reichert, instead of being librettists, became the German translators.
13 Franz Léhar (1870–1948) was the composer of the extremely successful operetta *The Merry Widow* which was first staged some ten years earlier.

Puccini revised it. Its reception in Vienna, after the end of the War, was lukewarm. He revised it again, almost to back to the original version. He hoped that it would do well in London, because the subject was a moral one (which the British tend to like), and it is melodious. But Covent Garden refused to accept it unless the text was lightened up with some comic dialogue, and it was given a happy ending. Puccini would not do this. It only reached the London stage in 1965.

La Rondine is the least successful of Puccini's mature works. The dialogue in act 1 is complicated, wordy and difficult to grasp. The behaviour of Lisette, the saucy maid, is improbable, and more perplexing than funny. The leading tenor Ruggero, who only has a single aria, is a pathetic character compared with Verdi's Alfredo. The hasty separation of the two lovers in act 3, which brings the evening to a rapid end, is unconvincing, and, most surprisingly for an opera of Puccini, the audience is left cold, and devoid of sympathy for the prima donna. The overall result is neither a sentimental comedy, nor a tragedy.

That said, Magda, has a very demanding and exciting part, much more so than in operetta generally: she has a 'good tune', *Chi il bel sogno di Doretta*, in which she describes her first passionate kiss. She has several high Cs. The opera also contains many attractive waltzes, 'drawing room' pieces, consistent with its setting in the period of the Second Empire. Even though anachronistic, there is also a slow foxtrot (*Perchè mai cercate*), a polka and an item in tango rhythm.

The root problem is the plot. Puccini, after *Edgar*, was normally meticulously careful about his plots. *La Rondine* is the exception which proves the rule.

Who's Who and What's What:

La Rondine

This summary is based on the libretto. As mentioned in the Warning at the end of this book, certain directors may amend opera stories to suit their production.

This portrayal of many different types of 'love' opens in the salon of **Magda** de Civry in Paris, during the Second Empire.[14] She is courtesan 'kept' by **Rambaldo** Fernandez.

Over coffee, which is served by her pert maid **Lisette**, the philosopher-poet **Prunier** has announced that sentimental love has become fashionable again. Three girls of doubtful virtue[15] mock him; Lisette, who aspires to be a stage-star, thinks he is talking nonsense.

Prunier is pleased that Magda takes his theme more seriously. It is fatal for 'Doretta', the character in his latest poem, which he begins to declaim, despite Rambaldo dismissing the topic as trite. In this unfinished work, 'Doretta' dreams that she refuses a king because his riches will not bring her happiness. Prunier invites the others to suggest an ending. Who can interpret Doretta's dream?

Magda picks up the challenge in her version of *Chi il bel sogno di Doretta?* In this well-known 'best-tune', she describes her first taste of passion, the naughty kiss she 'stole' from a penniless student. She then experienced true love, for which wealth has no relevance.

Prunier suggests that everybody has within them a romantic urge which is immensely powerful. Rambaldo, Magda's protector, proceeds to try to stifle this with a gift of a pearl necklace. But, whereas for Magda wealth does not buy happiness, for the other less well-placed girls, money is a requisite.

***

Lisette announces that the son of a childhood friend of Rambaldo has arrived.

Magda is reminded of the night she spent at Bulliers, the night-club, having escaped the clutches of her aunt: the youth, the drinks, caution

---

14 The Second Empire, of Napoleon III, was from 1852 until his defeat in the Franco-Prussian War of 1870.
15 The three girls are Yvette, Bianca and Suzy. Rambaldo's friends are Crébillon, Périchaud and Gobin. None of these parts is a distinct role.

flung to the winds – but also of a voice warning her that kisses and laughter had to be paid for with tears. She ran away. She longs to relive that couple of hours again.

Prunier feigns to be unimpressed, so Magda wonders what attracts a woman to him. The palms of their hands will reveal whether she has the necessary qualities, he explains. Like a fortune teller, he asks for a screen to be set up so that there can be a secluded corner. Magda offers herself.

***

Lisette shows in **Ruggero** Lastouc, who reminds her immediately of that youth in the night-club. Prunier meanwhile is reluctant to disclose his findings beyond a prediction that, like a swallow, *Forse come la rondine*, Magda will fly beyond the sea, in search of true love, and return again.

Ruggero wants to experience Paris night-life. Where better than in Bulliers? There amid all the hubbub, he will find passionate love.

The guests go off leaving Magda alone. She herself suddenly resolves to go to Bulliers on a nostalgic trip down memory lane.

***

Meanwhile Lisette – it is her night off – has changed into one of her boss's fashionable outfits and goes off with Prunier! His show of disliking of her was pretence. He loves her in his own particular way.

Magda returns. She is dressed as a grisette,[16] and almost completely unrecognisable.

***

The second act opens in Bulliers, a hubbub of activity of the demi-monde.[17] When Magda appears she is pestered by students, and takes refuge at a table at which Ruggero is sitting. This starts their romance. She tries to re-live that original experience. They express their love for each other. They dance; they kiss passionately. The students decide that they must not interrupt them.

Lisette and Prunier arrive and recognise Magda. Rambaldo, her lover, suddenly appears. Magda asks Prunier to get Ruggero out of the way.

16 Grisettes were the working-class girls of Paris, such as Mimì in *La Bohème*. Their background, denoted by the customary grey dress which they wore, enhanced their sexuality.
17 The girls include Georgette, Gabriella and Lolette; the students include Rabonier. None of these parts is a distinct role.

Rambaldo confronts Magda. He will tolerate a little adventure: but, 'time's up' and they should now go. But she says that she is leaving him. He says that he hopes that she does not regret it. She feels as if she is in a dream.

**

The third act opens in the South of France. Ruggero and Magda have flown off to the Côte d'Azur. There are swallows flying around.

She is taken aback when Ruggero reveals that he has written to his father to ask him to help with their expenses. He has also asked for permission to marry Magda. He passionately wants to live with her 'for ever' in the romantic countryside, where they can have a child. Magda is reminded of the voice warning that her romance had to be paid for with tears.

Lisette and Prunier have come to search for her. Lisette's attempt to become a star singer has crashed hopelessly, and she wants to return to her old job as a maid.

The **butler** allows them in.

Prunier tells Magda that, just as Lisette has surrendered her illusions, so should she. He has been asked to say this to her, by somebody who is very concerned for her.

Ruggero rushes in clutching a letter from his mother, who writes that, if his fiancée is virtuous, she will be glad to welcome her into the family. Magda blurts out that she has a 'past', she is *contaminata*. She must leave him, now.

He is overcome with disappointment. For her, Ruggero is the only man who has ever reached into her soul; but like a mother to her son, she must now say farewell. He can return to his house in the country. Like the swallow, she must fly back on her sorrowful way. She hopes that he will not forget her.

Lisette comes to support her, as she leaves. Ruggero is distraught.

TALKING POINTS: LA RONDINE

Giacomo Puccini (1858–1924)
Please see the summary of the life of Puccini on pages 159 and 160.

Puccini's Place as a Composer – a View
The view expressed on pages 161-163 is very relevant.

Courtesans
We learn in act 1 of *La Rondine* that Magda is a 'kept woman'. She is maintained as a mistress by Rambaldo, who produces a gift of a pearl necklace to add lustre to her routine.

Magda was at the top of the remuneration structure, and could feign indifference to the pearls. A really successful prostitute, the courtesan, the *grande horizontale* such as her, could select her clients to whom she would sell her warmth and award the trophy.

For others, it was different. Her friends, the tarts, the grisettes, Yvette, Bianca and Suzy, find that money is hard to come by. Indeed, for many in Paris, the oldest profession was the only escape from sheer economic desperation and starvation. The common prostitute who walked the streets with a bare bum under her silk skirt, might charge fifty centimes. A very high-class tart might charge say forty francs for the 'standard time' of between twelve to twenty minutes, or even a hundred francs when more adventurous tastes were catered for.

By contrast, 'La Païva', the mistress of the piano virtuoso and composer Henri Herz, climbed from the Moscow ghetto to a house in Paris with an alabaster staircase worth a million francs, and a bed for business said to have cost one hundred thousand francs. This was at a time when a skilled laundry-girl, who might carry on work until three in the morning, might earn three francs a day.

Liszt had an affair with Marie Duplessis, the model for Violetta in *La Traviata* which was based on *La Dame aux Camélias*, the novel by Alexandre Dumas (1824–1895), the son of the author of *The Three Musketeers*.

The similarity to La Traviata
La Rondine has been called 'the poor man's *La Traviata*'. 'The Lady with the Camellias' told of the twenty-five year-old Armand's love affair with

Marguerite, 'a virgin who some accident had made a courtesan', and who was always to be seen carrying a bouquet of camelias, 'a pale, scentless, cold flower, but sensitive as purity itself'. During the last five days of every month, she wore red ones.

There are considerable similarities between Magda and Dumas's Marguerite, *La Rondine* and *La Traviata*. Puccini's Magda is fortunate to be healthier than Verdi's Violetta: *La Traviata* ends with her dying of consumption. Ruggero, who must be one of the real wets of opera, is a naïve and innocent country-boy version of Dumas's Armand and Verdi's Alfredo.

Both operas begin with a party (and a fortune-teller or gypsies) at the courtesan's house, before the lovers escape to the countryside with little or no cash. There, in both operas, the affair comes to a halt as a consequence of parental intervention: a letter from Ruggero's mother persuades Magda to renounce her love; a visit from Alfredo's father Germont leads Violetta to give up Alfredo.

The notion of a courtesan actually falling in love with one of her men was not new: in Shakespeare's *Othello*, it was said of a courtesan: ''Tis the strumpet's plague to beguile many, and be beguil'd by one.'

ACT BY ACT: LE VILLI

Originally this was a one act opera. It contains the standard introductory chorus, and the prayer (Preghiera), a feature of nineteenth century opera. It had to comply with the entry conditions for the Sonzogno Prize for one-act operas, so the story was highly compressed. There was no room for scenes which might have been very 'operatic', for example the fleshpots of Mainz.

Puccini filled the gap with his symphonic intermezzo in which the orchestra, with the help of a narrator, describes the intervening events. This intermezzo is in two parts, The Desertion, describing Anna's grief and death, (which was staged with a funeral scene performed behind the gauze curtain), and The Witches' Sabbath, for the lively ballet of the Villi. Puccini did not have much choice about these arrangements. But the considerable orchestral involvement, including the introductions and ends to the arias and ensembles, led Verdi to warn that, taken to excess, this could be a bad thing.

Act 1

At the start of the prelude, we hear a haunting little phrase, a motive associated with the immutability of Roberto's vow of fidelity, which will recur in his duet with Anna in act 1, to the words *Dubita di Dio*. It recurs, ironically, at the end of the opera when his assurance has been shown to be hollow. In the Prelude, we also hear melody from *O sommo Iddio*, Roberto's prayer in act 2.

In spring-time in the Black Forest, in South Germany, mountaineers and villagers join in a betrothal party outside the cottage of Guglielmo Wulf. They are celebrating the betrothal of his daughter Anna to Roberto who has recently inherited a fortune from a rich woman in Mainz. He is going there to collect it.[18] There are great festivities, and even the sprightly old Guglielmo is persuaded to join in the dancing.

Anna, carrying a bouquet of forget-me-nots, expresses her apprehension: *Se come voi piccina io fosse*. If she were small like the flowers, she could always be near her beloved, and remind him not to forget her. She gives him the bouquet to take away.

Roberto joins her, and asks for a smile, because she is so sad. She tells him that she cannot stop weeping, because she has a premonition that she

18 The story in outline is similar to that of *The Rake's Progress,* depicted in a series of paintings by the eighteenth century English artist William Hogarth, and the basis of an opera by Stravinsky.

will never see him again. She even dreamt that she died while awaiting his return. He brushes all this aside. He professes his undying love for her: they have a wonderful future ahead of them. They have been childhood sweethearts, even when he was poor. He urges her not to doubt his love, because he loves her: doubt God, but do not doubt his love, *Dubita di Dio, ma no, dell'amor mio non dubitar*. She says she will engrave these words on her heart, and repeat them always.

They are rejoined by the others who urge Roberto to be on his way. The couple kneel before her father Guglielmo who blesses them, *Angiol di Dio*. They pray a pilgrim's prayer, that the journey will be successful; and that their dream of love will not fade away.

Roberto goes on his way.

* * *

There is a two-part intermezzo with orchestral music accompanying a Narrator, who speaks and does not sing. In the first part, the Desertion, *L'Abbandono*, the Narrator describes how, in Mainz, a whore lured Roberto into the fleshpots. He forgot his beloved. She waited for him, but at the end of winter she died of grief. The Chorus of women describes her in her coffin, as white as a cut lily-flower, her face as pale as moonlight.

The second part of the intermezzo is The Witches' Sabbath, Walpurgis Night, *La Tregenda*. The Narrator tells the legend of the 'Willis' who terrify unfaithful lovers. In the Black Forest, in the moonlight, the ghost of the jilted girl awaits the man who deserted her. If he comes, the Willis will surround him and dance him to death.

After Roberto's woman discarded him, he wanted to return home.

Act 2
On a freezing snowy winter's night the Willis dance around with imps and goblins. Guglielmo bewails the loss of his daughter who was happy until Roberto entered their lives: *No, possibil non è che invendicata*, a number which is much admired. He and his family had done nothing to deserve such treatment. It must be avenged. He calls to the spirit of Anna, *Anima santa della figlia mia*. If the Willis can await Roberto and avenge her, then he will be able to die contentedly. He craves the Lord's mercy for his unforgiving sentiments.

The Willis can be heard in the distance preparing to take revenge on Roberto. He returns to Anna's home, and crosses the bridge nearby. He sings a sequence which, it has been suggested, is possibly the longest solo

147

scene in all Italian opera, *Ecco la casa*. In this, the orchestra portrays the emotions, passion and despair, to an extent which Verdi's adherents criticised for drowning the tenor voice. It is terrible night with strange voices. Roberto does not think that he is haunted by the Willis, but by his own remorse. He thinks back to the happy days of May, when love bloomed: *Torna ai felice*. Now all is sadness and terror.

He wonders if Anna is alive, and goes to knock at the door of the house, but some force prevents him from doing so. He tries to pray: *O sommo Iddio del mio cammino*, a piece of which Puccini was proud, using it in the prelude to act 1 and the choral prayer. With her forgiveness, he could die in peace. But he cannot pray.

He curses the whore for whom he fell. He hears the sound of Anna's voice, but she no longer represents 'love', but 'revenge'. She describes how from their childhood they had enjoyed happiness and kisses together, *Tu dell'infanzia mia;* how he had urged her not to doubt his love, *Dubita di Dio, ma no, dell'amor mio non dubitar.* But he betrayed her. She lost hope, and died.

He realises that he destroyed her. He feels that he is near to death. Anna draws him towards her. The Willis dance around him, spinning and turning. He cannot escape: Anna will not let him go, but forces him to join the frenzied dance. He falls dead of exhaustion at her feet. You are mine, she declares, *Sei mio!* The Willis rejoice.

Act By Act: Edgar

Act 1

The opera opens near Courtray (Kortrijk) in Flanders, in 1302. There is a pleasant pastoral scene in a village nearby. It is April; dawn is rising. Edgar is asleep in front of the tavern. Peasants leave for the fields. Fidelia, offstage, hails the dawn, *O fior del giorno*, in a beautiful lilting melody. She has broken a bough off the almond tree to give Edgar as a morning greeting. And then she rushes off.

Peasant women arrive. But the peace is interrupted by Tigrana who has a lute strung around her shoulder. She is introduced by her motive, a raucous din, in total contrast to the pastoral scene. She is sarcastic about what she sees. She did not think that Edgar had a taste for pastoral love, but preferred something more raunchy and wild: gambling and sex. (People can be seen going to church behind them.) She tells him that he should go to church. He tries to resist her, to shut her up. She just laughs. The music is marked 'allegro satanico'.

Frank, Fidelia's brother, appears, in a tremendous rage. He was waiting for Tigrana last night. But she did not turn up: she finds him a bore. She says that, fifteen years ago, she was abandoned as a baby by the Moors. Frank says that they nurtured a viper in their midst. Tigrana agrees contemptuously that he should not be seen with her if he values his reputation.

In a fine, even if somewhat pathetic, aria, Frank wishes that he could escape from the love of Tigrana which has ensnared and bewitched him, *Questo amor, vergogna mia*. He is infatuated with her.

While the peasants continue to go into church, Tigrana interrupts with a sarcastic, contemptuous song, which she accompanies on her lute. It is about a lamb being devoured by a vulture. In some fine choral music above which she soars, the peasants try to drive her away. But she does not care a damn. She despises their accusation that she is a blasphemer and a whore. They condemn her for bringing death and disaster upon them.

Edgar comes. When the peasants say that she mocked them, they are amazed that he defends her; and tells them to go back to their prayers. He is leaving, making a complete break, and torching his house. He embraces Tigrana, and leaves with her for a life aflame with sensual pleasure.

Frank tries to prevent Tigrana leaving with Edgar: *T'arresta*. At first, Gualtiero, the father of Frank and Fidelia, intervenes and orders them to desist. In an impressive chorus, everybody agrees. When Edgar and

Tigrana again are about to go, *Or dunque, addio*, Frank again stops him, and they fight. Frank is wounded; he is about to strike Edgar when he is disarmed by Gualtiero. Edgar and Tigrana run off, but are cursed by Frank.

Act 2

It is nighttime in the garden of Edgar's castle, people (offstage) are enjoying sensual pleasure, for 'tomorrow we die': *Splendida notte.* Edgar comes out, to a beautiful haunting tune. He is not enjoying it: *Orgia, chimera.* He is afraid of 'tomorrow'. He longs to get out of the abyss into which he has sunk since that happy April, *O soave vision*, O sweet vision.

Tigrana interrupts him. She realises that he loves her no more, *Edgar, sulla fronte.* She has given him the lecherous life for which he longed. He has burnt his past, and there is nothing for him to return to. If he gives it up, he will be a beggar. She alone is his hope; they are inextricably joined together. He tries to repel her, while realising that he is hopelessly ensnared. Fate has united them and he cannot avoid the consequences. *Ah Edgar, dal labbro mio suggi l'oblìo.*

Martial trumpets are heard, and the noise of soldiers on the move. Edgar has an idea: he wants to see the captain. It turns out to be Frank. He asks for forgiveness. His sword cured him of a shameful love, *d'un amore abbietto, indegno.* Only Frank can be the means of his redemption: he can be redeemed if he joins and fights by Frank's side. Tigrana, who once was Frank's woman, pleads with him not to take Edgar away. But Edgar breaks free. He dedicates himself just to glory, and goes off to fight with the army. Tigrana says that he will either be hers, or die. It is her turn now to swear vengeance.

Act 3

We are to assume that Edgar and Frank went off to war and fought like brothers in arms, in Edgar's case with great heroism. Although he is assumed to have been killed, he has actually survived. A sham funeral has been arranged with full military honours: there is actually no corpse in the suit of armour lying on the catafalque. At this event, instead of glorifying him, Edgar, disguised as a monk, will highlight and denounce his own failings.

It is sunset. There is a sad, beautiful orchestral prelude, almost a funeral march, introducing the obsequies about to be held at a fortress near Courtray.

Monks, soldiers and people sing an atmospheric and masterly

Requiem[19] for the fallen hero, the dead soldier who they believe is Edgar, he who fought, for the love of his country and to prevent Flanders being enslaved. They too will fight for the cause and avenge his death.

A Monk (actually Edgar in disguise) accompanies Frank. Fidelia, griefstricken, and Gualtiero are part of the cortège.

Fidelia approaches the catafalque on which the body of Edgar lies in armour. She sings her fine lament, a Farewell, *Addio mio dolce amor.* She will be faithful unto death. In time, she will join him. The people and soldiers declare that Edgar's fame will never die.

Frank moves forward to begin his funeral oration, in which he praises Edgar's loyalty to his country, and his honour: *Del prode Edgar.*

The Monk (Edgar himself) however interrupts and draws attention to Edgar's failings. He recalls that Edgar broke with his past, set his family house ablaze, and lived in fleshpots. The others urge the Monk to be quiet. Frank presses on and praises Edgar's military glory in the cause of freedom. However, the Monk points out that Edgar was just a soldier of fortune, and had nothing to lose, so his valour was worthless. The soldiers and people are persuaded to hear more.

The Monk explains that, as Edgar lay dying, he ordered him to reveal his sins, as a sign of penitence and as an example. The Monk reminds the people that Edgar scorned and insulted them, he wounded Frank and went off with Tigrana, he gambled. So he was a wicked man. (Gualtiero quietly suggests to Fidelia that they should leave.) Worst of all, there was a wood beside his castle, in which travellers were known to have died. Or were murdered? Shame on him. His body should be thrown to the crows.

The crowd is about to attack the catafalque. But Fidelia stops them: *Non più! Fermate!* (The Monk regards her as a holy angel for defending him in this way.) No, she will not see the man she once loved insulted like this. That would be worse than anything: *D'ogni dolor questo è il più gran dolor.* She came from his village. He sinned. So what? He paid the price with his blood and his valour. She will take him back to her village cemetery, where he will await her in due course. The soldiers should bow their heads to their valiant captain.

Frank tells the people to leave. There is a beautiful orchestral interlude while they move off. Fidelia spreads laurel leaves and flowers on the coffin,

19 Toscanini conducted a performance of the Requiem at Puccini's own funeral. It is a wholly original piece, derived from Puccini's *Capriccio sinfonico*. One can understand why Puccini was so highly regarded at the Milan Conservatoire.

and eventually and reluctantly leaves.

***

Tigrana appears. She has come to mourn. But the Monk (Edgar) suspects that she just wants to make a show of grief. Frank is more charitable: he says that if she showed real pity, then he would support her. She declares emphatically that she has lost her loved one.

Frank asks Edgar to put her to the test, to see whether she is being hypocritical. He does this, in a beautiful melody: *Bella signora.* When he implores her to save her knees which are being bruised on the hard ground, she protests that she wants to pray. Frank approaches her and says that he wishes he were the dead man, because she would be mourning him. One pearl of her tears is worth a thousand pearls of a necklace, which he shows her. They press her to accept the necklace and jewels, and she almost yields. She wonders why they are tempting her so forcefully. One perjured word from her red lips will be enough, *Un ditto sol detta tua bocca vermiglia*, and the necklace will be hers. She hesitates, and under great pressure especially from Edgar, who appears satanic, and certainly far from monastic, she eventually yields to temptation: *Vincesti!*

The trumpets call the soldiers. The Monk declares that he denied Edgar an honourable burial. 'Now let Tigrana, Edgar's lover, speak.' She will confirm that Edgar was going to betray his country. He whispers to her that in return for this, she can have the jewels.

The soldiers, appalled, are about to throw his body to the crows, when they find that the there is no corpse in the armour.

The Monk reveals himself as Edgar, alive. Fidelia rushes to embrace him. He declares himself redeemed. He curses Tigrana, 'the scum of the earth, with her face of bronze and mud', *O lebbra, sozzura del mondo, o fronte di bronzo a di fango!* He will crush her.

Tigrana moves stealthily through the crowd and stabs Fidelia. Edgar and Frank go for Tigrana. Edgar falls sobbing on Fidelia's body, while the others drag Tigrana away to be killed.

ACT BY ACT : LA RONDINE

Act 1

It is after sunset, in Paris during the Second Empire. The act is set in the elegant salon of Magda de Civry, another of Puccini's 'girls of doubtful virtue'. She is kept by Rambaldo Fernandez.

The pert maid Lisette is serving coffee which Magda has poured out. Yvette, Bianca and Suzy, other girls of the same origin, are chatting up and mocking Prunier, a pompous philosopher-poet.[20] He has just opined that sentimental love, (kisses sighs and all that, *ma niente piu*, but nothing more)[21] has again become fashionable in Paris.

Lisette, who might be expected not to speak until spoken to, calls this nonsense. Men just say 'I want you'; the reply is 'OK'; and that's that. Prunier takes offence, and Magda excuses Lisette – who has pretensions to leave domestic service and become an actress – but tells her to leave the room.

Yvette, Suzy and Bianca parody sentimental love. But Magda takes it more seriously. This pleases Prunier.

Crébillon, a friend of Rambaldo, and his other friends (Périchaud and Gobin) take no notice, but talk about the latest news. Prunier warns them that sentimental love is like a disease: it is fatal for 'Doretta'. Who is that? She is the character in his latest poem. She has caught the disease.

The other press him to tell them about Doretta. Magda announces that he is going to declaim his poem about love. Rambaldo dismisses the subject as overexposed. Still, Prunier is pressed to declaim it, which he proceeds to do.

Who can interpret Doretta's dream? *Chi il bel sogno di Doretta*. It is a mystery. The king tried to seduce a girl with riches, but she said 'no' because gold cannot bring happiness. *Nient'altro che denaro*.

Prunier has not completed his poem, and he challenges the others to suggest an ending. As darkness falls, Magda picks up the challenge. She takes over at the piano: she describes how she escaped the clutches of an old aunt; she went out and met a student who kissed her on the mouth. The kiss gave her the first taste of passion. She then learnt about true love,

---

20 Prunier was the name of the *haute cuisine* restaurants in Paris and London founded in the 1870s by a distinguished chef.
21 Bianca instances the love exemplified in the romantic poetry of Alfred de Musset, who was himself very promiscuous. See the author's *Enchantress of Nations: Pauline Viardot, Soprano, Muse and Lover.*

reckless, intoxicating love, one of the greatest treasures on earth. Money has no measure in comparison with this type of love. That is her 'dream', as she reaches top C.

Prunier strews roses around her, and declares that in the heart of every soul, there is a romantic devil, a force more powerful than anything else. Everyone compliments her, including, surprisingly, Rambaldo, her protector. Magda is surprised that he is not disconcerted. But he suggests that he has the means of dispelling this devil. He presents her with a gift of a pearl necklace. Magda says that it does not change what she feels: this does not surprise him. Prunier, as an aside, says that his Doretta was not fazed by her situation, but he reckons that Magda may be.

* * *

Lisette hurries in, characterised by bitonal quavers (eighth notes) played in the orchestra. She tells Rambaldo that a visitor is pressing her to come in: he has already been waiting outside for a couple of hours and has already been back seven times. It turns out that he is the son of a childhood friend of Rambaldo.

Prunier again suggests that Lisette is intolerable, but Magda says that she, with her plans to be a great actress, provides a ray of sunshine in her dreary life. The other girls are surprised by Magda's attitude to the gift: for Suzy and Bianca, money is hard to come by. It does not buy happiness, says Magda.

They will, she suggests, always look back nostalgically to their days as grisettes, roaming freely among students and seamstresses. Oh, that she could re-live those days. She can vividly recall escaping from her aunt and spending the night at Bulliers. There was a man. To an exquisite waltz tune, which will recur later in the opera, she recalls a voice warning her that kisses and laughter had to be paid for with tears. He bought a couple of drinks with a gold coin, and told the waiter to keep the change. He asked her name. She wrote it down on the table; and he wrote down his next to hers. They gazed at each other, but, with the music suddenly becoming sad, she took fright, and ran away. That was it.

If only she could relive that moment again.

And what qualities does Prunier expect a woman to have? She must be a Cleopatra, a Camille, a Mona Lisa, a Salome. (There is a quote from Strauss's *Salome*.) How do you discover if she has them? By examining the palm of her hand. Magda offers 'have a go'. He asks for a screen to be set up so that there can be a secluded corner where he can demonstrate what he means.

* * *

154

Lisette brings Ruggero Lastouc in. He presents a letter of introduction. While Rambaldo reads it, the orchestra reveals the emotions running through Magda's mind, thoughts of student love. Prunier meanwhile is reluctant to disclose his findings: she will, like a swallow, *Forse, come la rondine*, fly beyond the sea, searching for love. But he refrains from disclosing the rest of his fortune-telling.

Ruggero tells Rambaldo about the excitement of being in the capital for the first time, Paris the city of desire. For a lad up from the country, the experience is overwhelming; everything is swept away in the agitation of desire. He asks Rambaldo to recommend where he should go; Rambaldo asks Prunier, who says 'to bed'.

He adds that the myth about the thrill of first day in Paris is so much nonsense. But Lisette interrupts and denies this. She is a Parisienne, and she defends the kingdom of women: Paris is full of charm. Despite Prunier trying to shut her up, Lisette says that the first evening in Paris is as exciting as seeing the sea for the first time. Rambaldo asks where they should send Ruggero. There are various suggestions such as the Moulin Rouge, Café Momus, Maxims – to some music with a suggestion of a Polka. But Lisette recommends Bulliers, where, amid all the hubbub, Ruggero should find passionate love. Off he goes. Magda throws the necklace on the table.

The guests go off leaving Magda alone. There is a short interlude, a waltz.

Lisette comes to remind her that it is her evening off.

Magda stops to ponder Prunier's prophesy, that, like a swallow, she would fly towards the sun, towards a land of dreams. She looks at the piece of paper on which Ruggero has scribbled the names of nightclubs. She suddenly resolves to go to Bulliers herself.

***

Lisette meanwhile has changed, without permission, into one of Magda's smart outfits and goes off with Prunier! (They continue to provide a comic element; but add to the complexity of the story.)

Prunier ardently professes his love for her: he had had to maintain a pretence of disliking her. A poet like him is expected only to love rich women. He does not like her hat, so she goes to change it. While she does this, he prays to the nine muses to forgive him, but he loves her so much. He advises her on her make-up and kisses her. They go off.

155

Magda comes in dressed as a grisette, almost completely disguised. Who can interpret Doretta's dream? *Chi il mistero di Doretta potè indovinar?* We hear the love theme. Magda is so well disguised that she is confident that nobody will ever guess who she is. No one will recognise her.

Act 2

Bulliers is full of students, artists, grisettes, prostitutes, flower girls milling around. Drink is flowing, and the place is lively, as the music, marked *Allegro energico*, indicates. Georgette runs a finger down a young man's shirt and asks if the pearl is real. She and Gabriella eye a young man. They try to seduce Ruggero who is sitting alone. Lolette wants to borrow some powder.

Magda appears. People wonder who this beauty can be, *Chi e?* She is pestered by the students.

She notices Ruggero and escapes towards him. She just wants to perch until the crowd has stopped pestering her. But he asks her to stay. For him, she is more like the girls back home in Montauban, down towards the Pyrenees. She wishes she could dance like them. This gives him the opening to ask her to dance. They go to the floor and get lost in the dance: *Nella dolce carezza*, a 'piece of genuine poetic feeling, whose gentle undulating line in euphonious thirds calls to mind the Flower music of Butterfly'. She feels that she is living the dream. Out in the garden, they are lost in the crowd also singing of kissing and its joys, in the springtime of love.

Prunier comes in with Lisette. He says that he will teach her how to improve herself.

Magda and Ruggero return exhausted from dancing and order two drinks, *Che caldo*. She tells him, as if re-living her dream, to give the waiter a gold piece and to keep the change. When she toasts love life, he is disconcerted. When he falls in love, it will be 'for ever'. They still do not know each other's names or anything about each other. He is Ruggero; she writes down 'Paulette' on the marble table top. There is no need for him to know anything about her. He should accept her just as she is, *Perchè mai cercate*. He realises that she is the girl of his dreams. They kiss passionately. Rabonier and other students decide that they must not interrupt this.

Lisette and Prunier recognise Magda: *Dio, Lei!* She indicates that she wants them to keep quiet about it. Prunier asks Ruggero whether Lisette's advice has brought him luck. Their drink is served. They toast their love. Magda wishes that this moment of her dream would never end: *Bevo al tuo fresco sorriso.* Her dream is coming true, as Magda indicates on top C. In contrast, Prunier and Lisette express theirs in technical poetic terms. The two couples kiss passionately, and the crowd shower them with flowers and join in, in a beautiful chorus.

Rambaldo suddenly appears. Magda asks Prunier to get Ruggero out of the way. Ruggero and Lisette go outside. Rambaldo, despite Prunier's attempt to keep them apart, confronts Magda. He says that he will tolerate a little adventure: but, it's over and they should now go. But she says that she is staying: she loves Ruggero, and will love him for ever. He must leave her to her destiny, to where fate takes her. It's all over with him. He is stunned by this. She asks him to forgive her. He leaves, saying that he hopes she will not regret it.

Dawn rises, with the sound of a soprano in the distance: *Nella trepida luce d'un matin.* Ruggero returns; the others have gone; and its time to escort Paulette away. She loves him, but 'he does not know'. She is as if in a dream. They both close on top B; and the orchestra fades away.

Act 3

Ruggero and Magda have fled to the south, like the swallows. On the Côte d'Azur, they are taking tea in a summerhouse above the sea. And there are swallows flying around. They savour the sea air and the countryside. With the orchestra playing a waltz, she pours him tea, and says that she has a potion to make him happy; he is passionately in love with her. Their love started in a garden. So, still to a waltz rhythm, she showers him with rose petals.

After a passionate embrace, he tells her that he has a secret to tell her. He needed money to pay the expenses which he has run up, lots of bills. So, three days ago, he wrote to his father for money. In the letter, he also asked his father's permission to marry Magda. She is thunderstruck by this revelation. But he passionately wants her 'for ever' and to take her to his home in the country, with its orchard, the beautiful view with the ever-changing light: *Dimmi che vuoi seguirmi alla mia casa.* They can have a child, and have the protection of his mother. The orchestra reminds her of that moment in act 1 when she was thinking back to her time as a grisette: she recalled a voice warning her that romance had to be paid for with tears.

He goes off for a moment, and she suddenly realises the horror of her situation: she does not know what to say to him. Must she tell him?

At this moment, she is interrupted by the sound of Lisette and Prunier, who have come to search for her. Lisette is frightened, nervous, and upset because Prunier's attempt to make the chambermaid into a star singer has failed catastrophically, despite all his efforts to train her. She appeared on the stage at Nice; she can still hear the sound of the whistles and catcalls. He assures her that he will protect her, and that they can set up as lovers in that lovely oasis.

She sees the butler, the major-domo, who asks her if she is looking for her mistress. Prunier answers that he should tell Magda that a gentleman and a lady-friend from Paris are here to see her. This annoys Lisette who bickers with Prunier.

Magda appears. Prunier wonders how she is getting on. In Paris, 'they' are all saying that she must find it very boring being secluded among her daydreams. She gets angry with him, and asks what he is doing there. He explains that, now that it is clear that Lisette is never going to be a success on stage, he has brought her back to Magda to be a maid. Lisette asks if she can return to her old job.

Prunier tells Magda that, just as Lisette has given up her illusions, so should she. He has been asked to say this to her, by somebody who is very concerned to save her from her illusions. But before Prunier leaves, he has one question for Lisette: what time will she be free tonight? Ten o'clock. Lisette just wants to go back to her old way of life. She goes and changes into her maid's outfit.

With the theme from the opening bars of the opera, Ruggero rushes in excitedly: *Amore mio*. He is clutching a letter from his mother. Magda reads it, ashamed, *Figliuolo, tu mi dici*.

Ruggero's mother writes that if his fiancée is virtuous, she will be glad to welcome into the family the girl who is to be the mother of his children. She sends his bride a kiss. Magda is most discomfited; she blurts out that she cannot go on with this. She has a 'past' (we hear those opening chords again). She is not pure, she is *contaminata*. Shamelessly, she has traded her body for gold. She cannot go on deceiving him. She must leave him, now.

He is overcome with disappointment. He pleads with her: she will break his heart, *Ma come puoi lasciarmi*. Magda says that his mother needs him, and she must leave. Magda does not want to ruin him. But, he is the only man who has ever reached into her soul. Like a mother, she must now say farewell. He will return to his house in the country. Like a swallow, she must fly back on her sorrowful way. She hopes that he will not forget her.

Lisette comes to support her, as she departs. Ruggero is distraught.

PUCCINI-LIFE

Giacomo Puccini (1858-1924)

Puccini came from a musical family in Lucca, a city in Tuscany. He became a student at the Milan Conservatoire. (His early days and his slow start, are amplified in the background to *Le Villi*, his first opera, on page 129.) He entered *Le Villi* into a competition, but it was rejected, probably on account of the score being illegible. His next opera, *Edgar*, was not a success.

Puccini modelled himself on Massenet, France's most popular composer, a mass-producer of pleasing operas including *Manon*. Puccini also based his first successful opera *Manon Lescaut* on the novel by Abbé Prévost.

The prominent Milanese music publisher Giulio Ricordi cemented Puccini's partnership with the librettists Luigi Illica (1857 – 1919) and Giuseppe Giacosa (1847 – 1906), the 'holy trinity' as Ricordi called them – see pages 12 & 13. They had participated in the creation of *Manon Lescaut*, and with them, he composed *La Bohème* (1896), *Tosca* (1900) and *Madama Butterfly* (1904). Giacosa had died by the time that *La Fanciulla del West* followed in 1910. Puccini's remaining completed operas, *La Rondine* (1917) and *Il Trittico* (1918) were less remunerative.

At a time when the operatic heir to Verdi was being sought, the music critic and novelist George Bernard Shaw thought that Puccini, with his catching melodies, was the likely candidate. His main rivals, Mascagni and Leoncavallo, the composers of *Cavalleria rusticana* and *I Pagliacci* respectively, lacked sustainability.

Puccini portrays a realistic picture. His style is sometimes called 'verismo', a term applied to many of the pictures, novels and drama of the late nineteenth century. The dramatic and emotional element is uninhibitedly inflated. The protagonists are passionate and often jealous, vengeful, and violent, as in *Tosca* and *Il Tabarro* (the first component of *Il Trittico*). This style is redolent of Bizet's *Carmen*, which was premièred in 1875; and also of *Cavalleria rusticana*, which had been immensely successful, and applauded to an almost absurd extent. Puccini, together with these composers, contributes more than his fair share to the Hundred Best Tunes.

Puccini became concerned that he was growing out of touch with modern music. By the time of *Turandot*, the horrible character of the Chinese Princess justified him in imparting modern, dissonant and exotic sounds which we might not otherwise expect, or like, from him. Still, that opera also includes melody which we hum, as we leave the theatre, such as the aria *Nessun dorma*, sung by Pavarotti in one of the most famous recordings in classical music.

Puccini was a chain-smoker, who lived a 'fast' life and chased women. He took Elvira, his long-term mistress, off a school-friend. She could only marry him after her husband had died; this was nearly twenty years after she had borne Puccini a son.

He had a particularly unfortunate tryst with Doria Manfredi, a domestic servant at his house in Torre del Lago near Lucca. The 'affaire Doria' and the jealousy it aroused in Elvira, runs like an idée fixe through Puccini's later operas. It had a negative influence until it was seemingly exorcised with his music for the suicide of Liù, the slave girl, in *Turandot*.

Puccini's hobby was shooting birds, especially on Lake Massaciuccoli near his villa, quite close to Lucca. He also had a passion for high-speed motor cars, and was lucky to survive, with just a broken leg, a crash in which his car plunged down a steep embankment before turning over.

His unpatriotic attitude during World War I made him unpopular. Italy was divided. Puccini tried to stay neutral. He feared for the fate of his operas in Austria and Germany; besides, he disliked France where his operas were not well-received. The French Press attacked him.

He developed throat cancer, and died in a Brussels clinic on 24 November, 1924. At the time, he was still working on *Turandot*.[1] He had composed the music up to the death of Liù.

---

1 Further information on Puccini may be found in the author's *The Lives and Times of the Great Composers* (ebook and hardcopy) published by Icon Books Ltd.

PUCCINI'S PLACE AS A COMPOSER – A VIEW

Music was already undergoing a considerable revolution by the time Puccini wrote *La Bohème*, one of the most popular and effective operas today. Wagner was long dead, Debussy already had *Pelléas* in hand, Schoenberg was aged twenty-one and Stravinsky was thirteen. By the time he died in 1924, and bequeathed us his twelve operas, Puccini's style was an anachronism. As a consequence, he tends to get a bad press from musical professionals.

Fauré, who many know mainly as the composer of *The Requiem*, called *La Bohème* 'a dreadful Italian work'. 'I met Puccini twice,' Fauré wrote, a few years after attending a *Bohème* performance, 'I wasn't able to escape'. He disparaged the Paris première of *Tosca* as an important event because 'of the librettist, and the bizarre school of music to which the composer Puccini belongs. It consists of three or four chaps who have conjured up a neo-Italian art which is easily the most miserable thing in existence'. For Fauré, Puccini and his contemporaries Mascagni and Leoncavallo, the composers of *Cavalleria rusticana* and *Pagliacci*, produced 'a kind of soup, where every style from every country gets all mixed up. And everywhere, alas! they are welcomed with open arms'.

Puccini did respond to many of the changes to musical language being driven forward by other composers;[2] but, in many respects he was static, eclectic. So, if to be a great artist one must drive the art forward, then, he cannot be reckoned as one.

Puccini's operas cannot begin to claim the same stature as a piece of abstract instrumental music by (say) Beethoven, which is on a different intellectual level. But *Madama Butterfly* and *La Bohème* are numbers one and two in charts of top-performing operas, and *Tosca* is in the top ten. And *La Bohème* does not have the advantage of the American aspects to the *Madama Butterfly* story. Although popularity on its own is no measure of artistry, there comes a point where critics begin to look foolish and out of touch. Taunts about being bourgeois and commercial, and *Tosca* being 'a shabby little shocker', are more redolent of envy than objective criticism.

Puccini was a consummate craftsman. He had an extraordinary sense of theatre and of pace, he was very skilled in his use of the orchestra,

---

2 The atmosphere of *La Fanciulla del West* is set by the harsh opening bars of act 1; the act ends on a discord. In it, he makes use of the whole-tone scale, consisting of the six notes within the octave, each a whole tone apart. And he uses 'reminiscence motives', 'a sort of musical label', a snippet of melody which has already been heard in connection with the same subject matter (person, thing or emotion) – for example, in act 3, when Sheriff Jack Rance pictures Minnie in Johnson's arms. But his use of motives is not remotely as developed as Wagner's complex use of leitmotives.

and he could invent incandescent lyrical phrases and tunes. These skills combined to make the audience feel a heartfelt sense of compassion with his characters, whether Mimì, Butterfly, Suor Angelica, or even the whore Manon Lescaut.[3]

The theatrical 'Te Deum' scene which concludes act 1 of *Tosca*, with its procession and chorus, has been 'reckoned one of the most impressive finali in opera;' and, at the conclusion to *La Bohème*, so reminiscent of Violetta's death in Verdi's *La Traviata*, most in the audience are discomfited to find the lights are up before the handkerchief can be hidden away. Perhaps, however, there is an element of truth in the suggestion by an eminent musicologist that 'what was ardent passion on Verdi's stage became more like hysteria on Puccini's.'

Still, that hysteria provided a sense of pace, such that the drama never flags.[4] The final scene in *La Bohème* exemplifies this. Thus, despite being one of the best-known dying scenes ever produced on the stage, Mimì's death never becomes mawkish and its pace is sustained until the end.[5] The scene is so effective that it has become notorious. His sustaining of the tension in the final, dramatic scenes of *La Fanciulla del West* (for example) is also masterly.

We can observe his skilled use of the orchestra to create atmosphere: in *Il Tabarro* he evokes the atmosphere of Paris and the bargemen moored on the murky, misty River Seine. In *Turandot,* he drew on Chinese folk music and percussion, including xylophones, bells and gongs of various sizes. In *Madama Butterfly,* he quotes tunes from Japan, and evokes sounds and tunes in the 'Japanese manner', especially with bells, the woodwind and the use of high-pitched timbres. The thinness and simplicity of his orchestration enhances the exotic atmosphere. There is a world of difference between *Madama Butterfly* and a typical Italian opera such as Donizetti's *Lucia di Lammermoor,* which is set in Scotland but in which little is Scottish except the costumes.

Conventional opera audiences were disturbed by the role and weight increasingly being given to the orchestra, a trend labelled as 'Wagnerian' – a pejorative, depreciatory expression often used by Italians worried about the direction in which music was heading – even though the music might have none of the complexities or pretensions of Wagner's music.

Puccini's tendency to follow this trend was criticised from the start, with *Le Villi*. Singers also were unhappy with 'descriptive music in which

---

3 A reason for the failure of *La Rondine* is possibly the lack of sympathy that is generated for Magda, the courtesan.
4 Apart from, arguably, in *La Rondine*, which is part of 'its problem'.
5 The audience suspects the truth and is warned by Schaunard. But Rodolfo does not re-alise that Mimì is dead until Marcello, with great anguish cries out '*Corragio*' ('courage!').

they appear to do little more than mime'. Their status was being diluted.

Whereas the role of music in opera had, for long, been to complement the action on stage,[6] and thus assist members of the audience to experience a suitable personal emotional response,[7] Puccini did not just induce that response: he drove it like he drove his Clément-Bayard motorcar, fast and with little caution or subtlety.

Take for example act 2 of *Tosca*. We are presented with a man about to force himself upon a woman. The libretto invites us to wonder why she should deserve this? She has devoted herself to art and love; she has never meant to hurt anyone; she has contributed to church funds and attended its services. A theatre audience would perhaps experience a frisson of shocked excitement, even disgust at the commonplace scene which is portrayed. Puccini's music for the *Vissi d'arte* however heats up the potentially prosaic response of an opera audience to a temperature such that the experience provided is deeply moving and unforgettable: some might say that the temperature is 'dangerous', or 'unhealthy'.

This orchestral underpinning and, in addition, the emotional, often soaring, sensuously beautiful, melodies account for the popularity and lasting success of Puccini's music. We associate him with incandescent lyrical phrases, brief, simple and thus so memorable and hummable, such as *O soave fanciulla* in *La Bohème* or *O mio babbino caro* from *Gianni Schicchi*. We can recall sections of his operas, such as the glorious fifteen-minute *Che gelida manina* sequence which concludes act 1 of *La Bohème*. With the tenor holding a B flat and also achieving top C, its place, and Puccini's, in any 'All-time Hundred Best Tunes' is surely secure. Tosca's *Vissi d'arte*, and the *Nessun dorma* in *Turandot* are not far behind. Even the discredited *La Rondine* has its 'good tune', *Chi il bel sogno di Doretta*, the aria in which the prima donna describes her first passionate kiss. Like the kiss, the list is long, and lasting.

---

6 The relative weight assigned to music and words was a contentious issue grasped by many composers including Mozart and Richard Strauss.
7 By contrast, Wagner allowed no such latitude. He 'socks it to you, hook line and sinker' with his orchestral music. Orchestral sounds, including motives and themes already heard, are intended by him to provide his comprehensive explanation of events on stage, and explain the inner action. For some, this complete expression of passion and experience is responsible for the intoxication that Wagnerian music creates in the listener.

WARNING

In the Preface to the Volume One, *Great Operas – A Guide to 25 of the World's Finest Musical Experiences*, the author warned that the Guides cannot anticipate a particular production which does not conform to the composer's intentions.

Composers, from Berlioz to Debussy to Britten, have long deplored the attempts of those purporting to 'improve' on their work.

Especially recently, some operas have been hijacked by their producers. Sometimes, it is considered that the work, even just the overture, needs 'modernising' or sensationalising to attract and retain an audience's attention. So, time, place and story are adapted, perhaps to make some political or social point not intended by the composer. Puccini's operas have been prone to such cavalier treatment.

Often all this makes artistic nonsense of both music and text. Stage action may be crassly juxtaposed with music or specific musical themes, seemingly ignoring the composer's laboriously-worked musical design and intention. An inherent weakness of opera is exploited, in that many in the audience may not be proficient in the Italian in which it is being performed.

Of course, the castrati of eighteenth century opera are not to be found today. So, axiomatically, some alteration to opera, certainly as early as that of the baroque era, is always going to be necessary. In later periods, lengthy recitative may need cutting, if it is redundant. And, moving on, other adaptation, for example, dress and taking advantage of modern stage technology, may be justified and desirable artistically. But, any reckless or ill-considered alteration is objectionable and can be an indication of ignorance. The malpractice is extraordinary in an age which rightly demands authenticity. It tends to annoy, to anger and – worse – to distract.

The opera is not the producer's opera. It is the composer's opera. That balance must be maintained. To present it otherwise is a misrepresentation. It will be Puccini's opera, provided that the audience fairly judges that the production is one which he would approve of, if present to experience it with today's facilities.

Enjoy Puccini's opera!

ACKNOWLEDGEMENTS AND SOURCES

The author wishes to thank his wife Rosemary for her ideas, assistance and forbearance; and, particularly, among the many who have used or read drafts in the series, Dr Janie Steen, Dr Guy Deutscher, David Vaughan, Dr Jonathan Price, and Tom Allen for their specific advice. Dr Caitríona Ó Dochartaigh and Tom Kavanagh also gave very helpful advice and suggestions. The team at Icon Books (especially Andrew Furlow, and Duncan Heath) were very helpful as was Steven Weekes. Chris Shamwana designed the cover. Richard Todd helped with images, as did Susan Atkinson. Members of the family were very helpful and patient. Images, except as indicated otherwise, are from the author's own collection and/or, as in the case of those from the internet (for example, Wikipedia), were published before 1923 and are in the public domain in the US and most countries of the world.

To obtain information, the internet was generally only used as a secondary or confirmatory source.

Icon Books kindly gave permission to include chapters and text previously published by them. The cover image 'At the Opera' 1865 by T. F. Dicksee, © Leicester Arts & Museums/The Bridgeman Art Library, is from the New Walk Museum & Art Gallery, Leicester, UK.

Other image credits, where known:
Jeritza, M., *Sunlight and Song* (London: D. Appleton and Company 1924); Lina Cavalieri *New York Star* (January 30, 1909) Vol.1 No.118; Caruso 1910 postcard, no attribution; The Holy Trinity, and cartoon, De Agostini Picture Library/A Dagli Orti/Bridgeman Images; Callas, CSU Archives/Everett Collection/Bridgeman Images; Young Puccini, Lebrecht Music Arts/Bridgeman Images; Puccini with Belasco, Tully Potter/Bridgeman Images; Eva Turner, ©Richard Bebb Collection/Bridgeman Images; Callas and Gobbi, ©John Massey Stewart/Bridgeman Images; Sibyl Sanderson, Bibliothèque Nationale de France, 1888; Edgar by Giovanni Zuccarelli (1846–1897).

Manon Lescaut

Sources of quotes (some altd.):
Carner, M, *Puccini* (London: Duckworth, 1974. 2nd edition) pp. 56, 62, 64, 271, 317, 319, 320, 321, 325; *New Oxford Companion to Music* (ed. Denis Arnold) (Oxford: Oxford University Press, 1983) p. 1141, 1507; Grout, D., *A History of Western Music* (London: J.M.Dent & Sons 1962) p. 608; B. Shaw *Music in London 1890-94* (London: Constable, 1949) vol. iii pp. 220, 223; The score, Ricordi 1915 edition, flysheet, seriatim; Lang, P.H., *Music in Western Civilisation* (London: J. M. Dent and Sons Ltd, 1963) p. 1000; Gowan, C., *France from the Regent to the Romantics* (London: Harrap 1961) p. 49; *Encyclopaedia Britannica* ninth edition, vol. xix pp. 719, 720; vol. xv. p. 22; Prévost, Abbé. (intro P. Mac Orlan), *Manon Lescaut* (Librairie Génerale Française, 1959) pp.11,16, 35, 56, 177; Kobbé, G., *The Complete Opera Book* (London: G.P.Putnam's Sons, 1930) p. 737; *New Grove Dictionary of Music and Musicians* (ed. S. Sadie), (London: Macmillan, 1980) vol. 7, p. 346, Giacosa (W. Weaver); vol. 9, p. 25 Illica (W. Weaver); vol. 11, pp. 801, 802 Massenet (W.Carroll); vol. 15, Puccini (M Carner); Ducloux, W., in *Manon Lescaut libretto* (New York:

Franco Colombo Inc 1965); Douglas, N. *Legendary Voices* (London: André Deutsch, 1992), pp. 12, 31; Massenet, J., *Manon* (New York: Kalmus 1968) p. 128, 153; Richardson, J: *The Courtesans – the demi-monde in 19th century France*, Weidenfeld & Nicolson, London 1967.

Other sources:
Jenkins, G. & d'Antal, S., *Kiri* (Hammersmith: HarperCollins, 1998); *New Grove Dictionary of Opera* (ed. S. Sadie), (London: Macmillan, 1992) vol. 2, pp. 253, 403 (J. Budden); Irvine, D: *Massenet, a Chronicle of his Life and Times*, (Portland Oregon: Amadeus Press 1994) p.129; Steen, M., *The Lives and Times of the Great Composers* (Cambridge: Icon Books, 2003); Berlioz, H., (ed.) D. Cairns, *Memoirs*, (London: Sphere Books 1990) p. 55; Kildea, P., *Benjamin Britten* (London: Allen Lane 2013) p. 303; Nichols, R. and Lesure, F., (ed.) *Debussy Letters* (London: faber and faber 1987) p. 41; Tanner, M., *Wagner* (London: Flamingo 1997) p. 60; Steen, M., *Enchantress of Nations, Pauline Viardot, Soprano,Muse and Lover* (Cambridge: Icon Books, 2007).

La Bohème

Sources of quotes (some altd.):
Puccini, G., *La Bohème*, full score (Milan: Ricordi, 1999); Carner, M., *Puccini* (London: Duckworth, 1992. 3rd edition) pp. 86, 88, 93, 341, 342, 345; *Encyclopaedia Britannica* ninth edition, vol. xvii, p. 54; vol xviii, pp. 405 (pathology), 855, 858 (Phthisis); *New Grove Dictionary of Music and Musicians* (ed. S. Sadie), (London: Macmillan, 1980) vol. 15, Puccini (M. Carner) pp. 437, 435; Barrie Jones, J. (trans. and ed.) *Gabriel Fauré: A Life in Letters*(London: Batsford, 1988) p. 103; Lang, P.H., *Music in Western Civilisation* (London: J.M. Dent & Sons Ltd, 1963) pp. 999, 1000; Pavarotti, L. and Wright, W., *My World* (London: Chatto & Windus 1995) pp. 36, 37, 284; Hewlett-Davies, B., *A Night at the Opera* (London: Weidenfeld & Nicolson, 1980) p. 45; Atkins, H., and Newman, A., *Beecham Stories* (London: Futura 1983) p. 37; Breslin, H., and Midgette, A., *The King and I: Luciano Pavarotti's Rise to Fame* (Edinburgh: Mainstream Publishing, 2004) p. 175; McPhee, P., *A Social History of France 1789–1914* (Basingstoke: Palgrave Macmillan, 2004) pp. 130, 138, 141, 189.
Other sources:
Jenkins, G. and d'Antal, S., *Kiri* (London: HarperCollins, 1998); Mansel, P., *Paris Between Empires, 1814–1852* (London: John Murray, 2001); *New Grove op. cit.* vol. 7, Giacosa (W. Weaver); vol. 9 Illica (W. Weaver); Shaw, G.B., *Music in London 1890–94* (London: Constable, 1949); Vickers, H., *Even Greater Operatic Disasters* (London: Jill Norman & Hobhouse Ltd, 1982); Steen, M., *The Lives and Times of the Great Composers* (Cambridge: Icon Books, 2003) ch. 27; Lucas, J., *Thomas Beecham* (Woodbridge: The Boydell Press, 2008).

Tosca

Sources of quotes (some altd.):
Carner, M., *Puccini* (London: Duckworth, 1974 2nd edition) pp. 102, 110, 349, 364, 366, 369; Barrie Jones, J. (transl. and ed.), *Gabriel Fauré: A Life in Letters* (London: Batsford, 1988) p. 111; Lang, P.H., *Music in Western Civilisation* (London: J.M. Dent & Sons Ltd, 1963) p. 999; Stassinopoulos, A., *Maria* (London: Weidenfeld & Nicolson, 1980) pp. 138, 155, 220, 222; *New Grove Dictionary of Music and Musicians* (ed. S. Sadie), (London: Macmillan, 1980) Puccini (M. Carner) vol. 15, pp. 432, 435; Vandiver Nicassio, S., *Tosca's Rome: The Play and the Opera in Historical Perspective* (Chicago: University of Chicago Press, 2002) p. 2; Pavarotti, L. and Wright, W., *My World* (London: Chatto & Windus, 1995) pp. 35, 36, 72; Kobbé, G., *The Complete Opera Book* (London: G.P. Putnam's Sons, 1930) p. 662; Douglas, N., *Legendary Voices* (London: André

Deutsch, 1992), p. 222; (Nilsson, B., *La Nilsson*(Boston: Northeastern University Press, 2007) p. 69; Steen, M., *The Lives and Times of the Great Composers* (Cambridge: Icon Books, 2003) ch. 27.

Other sources:

Encyclopaedia Britannica ninth edition, vol. xvii, p 204; vol. xx, p. 806; *New Grove Dictionary of Opera*(ed. S. Sadie), (London: Macmillan, 1992) vol. 2, p. 893; Giacosa (W. Weaver); vol. 9, p. 25 Illica (W. Weaver); vol. 12, p. 765 Mugnone (C. Casini); Shaw, G.B., *Music in London 1890–94* (London: Constable, 1949) vol. iii, p. 220; Lebrecht, N., *The Book of Musical Anecdotes* (London: André Deutsch, 1985); Domingo, P., *My First Forty Years* (London: Weidenfeld & Nicolson, 1983); Vickers, H., *Great Operatic Disasters*(London: Macmillan, 1981); Jeritza, M., *Sunlight and Song* (London: D. Appleton and Company 1924) pp.176, 160; Vickers, H., *Even Greater Operatic Disasters* (London: Jill Norman & Hobhouse Ltd, 1982); Hewlett-Davies, B., *A Night at the Opera* (London: Weidenfeld & Nicolson, 1980); Jenkins, G. and d'Antal, S., *Kiri* (London: HarperCollins, 1998);*Times Literary Supplement*, 6 June, 2008, p. 7.

Madama Butterfly

Sources of quotes (some altd.):

Puccini, G., *Madama Butterfly* full score (San Giuliano Milanese: UMP Ricordi, 1999); Carner, M., *Puccini* (London: Duckworth, 3rd edition 1992), pp. 131, 136, 140, 142, 389, 392, 398; Barrie Jones, J., (trans. and ed.), *Gabriel Fauré: a Life in Letters* (London: Batsford, 1988) pp. 103, 111; Lang, P.H., *Music in Western Civilisation* (London: J.M. Dent & Sons Ltd, 1963) p. 999; Rutherford, S., *The Prima Donna and Opera 1815–1930* (Cambridge: Cambridge University Press 2006) p. 217; Kobbé, G., *The Complete Opera Book* (London: G.P. Putnam's Sons, 1930) p. 673; Stassinopoulos, A., *Maria* (London: Weidenfeld & Nicolson, 1980) p. 124; Hewlett-Davies, B., *A Night at the Opera* (London: Weidenfeld & Nicolson, 1980) p. 33; Allen, T., *Foreign Parts* (London: Sinclair-Stevenson 1993) pp. 126, 127.

Other sources:

Domingo, P., *My First Forty Years* (London: Weidenfeld & Nicolson, 1983); *New Grove*vol. 15, Puccini (M. Carner); vol. 7, p. 346, Giacosa (W. Weaver); vol. 9, p. 25, Illica (W. Weaver); Shaw, G.B., *Music in London 1890–94* (London: Constable, 1949) vol. iii;*Encyclopaedia Britannica* 9th edition, vol. xiii p. 581; Fowler, H., *A Dictionary of Modern English Usage*, (Oxford: Clarendon Press 1963) p. 295; Loti, P. (transl. C. Bell, intro. K. O'Connor), Tahiti, *The Marriage of Loti*, (London: KPI 1986) p. vii; Steen, M., *The Lives and Times of the Great Composers* (Cambridge: Icon Books 2003).

La Fanciulla del West

Sources of quotes (some altd.):

Verdi, G., *La Fanciulla del West in full score* (New York: Dover 1980); Carner, M, Puccini (London: Duckworth, 1974) pp. 187, 190, 202, 205, 275, 402, 405, 455; *New Grove Dictionary of Music and Musicians* (ed. S. Sadie), (London: Macmillan, 1980) vol. 15, p. 433 Puccini (M. Carner); Jenkins, G. & d'Antal, S., *Kiri* (Hammersmith: HarperCollins, 1998) p. 253; Domingo, P. *My First Forty Years* (London: Weidenfeld & Nicolson, 1983) p. 105.

Other sources:

New Grove Dictionary of Music and Musicians (ed. S. Sadie), (London: Macmillan, 1980) vol. 1, p. 309 Amato (D. Shawe-Taylor); vol. 5, p. 399 Destinn (D. Shawe-Taylor); Shaw, G. B., *Music in London 1890-94* (London: Constable, 1949) vol. iii, p. 220; Steen, M., *The Lives and Times of the Great Composers* (Cambridge: Icon Books, 2003) ch. 27; Nye, R B & Mopurgo, J: *A History of the United States*, (Harmondsworth: Penguin, 1965) p. 426); *Encyclopaedia Britannica* ninth edition, vol. iv, p.

694; Wilson, C, *Giacomo Puccini*, (London: Phaidon, 1997); *New Oxford Companion to Music* (ed. D. Arnold) (Oxford: Oxford University Press, 1983), p. 1621; Kobbé, G., *The Complete Opera Book* (London: G.P.Putnam's Sons, 1930); Oxford Paravia Italian Dictionary (Oxford University Press 2009) p. 1832; Noble, J., *The Jealous Demon, My Wretched Health* (Woodbridge: Boydell & Brewer Ltd, 2018) pp. 269, 355.

Il Trittico

Sources of quotes (some altd.):

Carner, M, *Puccini* (London: Duckworth, 1974. 2nd edition) pp. 36, 187, 216, 246, 258, 262, 266, 267, 284, 424, 425, 446, 447, 455; Dante Alighieri, (transl. C. Sisson, intro. D. Higgins) *The Divine Comedy* (Oxford: OUP 1993) pp. 46, 173, 563; Weaver, W. *Seven Puccini Librettos* (New York: Norton 1981) p. 387; *New Grove Dictionary of Music and Musicians* (ed. S. Sadie), (London: Macmillan, 1980) vol 15, Puccini (M. Carner) p. 434; Steen, M., *The Lives and Times of the Great Composers* (Cambridge: Icon Books, 2003) p. 823.

Other sources:

Lucas, T., *Thomas Beecham*, (Woodbridge: The Boydell Press 2008); Breslin, H., & Midgette, A., *The King and I, Luciano Pavarotti's rise to fame* (London: Mainstream Publishing, 2004); Domingo, P. *My First Forty Years* (London: Weidenfeld & Nicolson, 1983); Douglas, N. *Legendary Voices* (London: André Deutsch, 1992); Evans, G., *A Knight at the Opera* (London: Futura, 1985); *Il Tabarro*, (Milan: Ricordi vocal score, 1960); *Gianni Schicchi*, (Milan: Ricordi vocal score, 1957); *Suor Angelica*, (Milan: Ricordi vocal score, 1978); Parker, R., *Gianni Schicchi as a national monument* (Glyndebourne programme 2004); Shaw, G.B. *Music in London 1890-94* (London: Constable, 1949); (Gowan, C., *The Background of the French Classics* (London: George G. Harrap & Co. Ltd 1960); Walter, B, *Theme and Variations,* (London: Hamish Hamilton, 1947); *Encyclopaedia Britannica* ninth edition, vol. iv p. 19; *New Oxford Companion to Music* (ed. Denis Arnold) (Oxford: Oxford University Press, 1983); Kobbé, G., *The Complete Opera Book* (London: G.P.Putnam's Sons, 1930); Wikipedia.

Turandot

Sources of quotes (some altd.):

Puccini, G., *Turandot*, full score, (Milan: Ricordi, 2000); Carner, M., *Puccini* (London: Duckworth, 1992 3rd edition) pp. 172, 439, 465, 473, 479, 486, 488; Shakespeare, W., *The Merchant of Venice*, Act II sc. I; Pavarotti, L. and Wright, W., *Pavarotti, My World* (London: Chatto & Windus, 1995) p. 67; Breslin, H. and Midgette, A., *The King and I: Luciano Pavarotti's Rise to Fame* (Edinburgh: Mainstream Publishing, 2004) p. 208; Lebrecht, N., *The Book of Musical Anecdotes* (London: André Deutsch, 1985) p. 245; DiGaetani, J., *Carlo Gozzi: A Life in the 18th Century Venetian Theater* (Jefferson, North Carolina: McFarland & Company, Inc., 2000) pp. 4, 125, 127; Douglas, N., *Legendary Voices* (London: André Deutsch, 1992) p. 257; Nilsson, B., *La Nilsson* (Boston: Northeastern University Press, 2007) pp 89, 185, 188, 200; Domingo, P., *My First Forty Years* (London: Weidenfeld & Nicolson, 1983) p. 19; Chrysalia (pseudonym): *Calaf, A Rejected Drama* (London: T. Hookham, 1826) Act 1, pp. 13, 15, 17; Gozzi, C. (ed. A. Bermel and T. Emery), *Five tales for the Theatre* (Chicago: University of Chicago Press 1989) p. 1.

Other sources:

New Grove Dictionary of Music and Musicians (ed. S. Sadie), (London: Macmillan, 1980) vol. 1, p. 250 Alfano (J. Waterhouse); vol. 15, Puccini (M. Carner) pp. 437, 435; *Encyclopaedia Britannica* ninth edition, vol. xi, p. 24, vol. x, p. 759; Shaw, G.B., *Music in London 1890–94*

(London: Constable, 1949) vol. iii, p. 220; Stassinopoulos, A., *Maria* (London: Weidenfeld & Nicolson 1980 p. 181; Major, N., *Joan Sutherland* (London: Little Brown, 1993) p. 227; P. Casali, 'The Pronunciation of Turandot, Puccini's Last Enigma', *Opera Quarterly* (1997) vol. 13 no. 4 pp. 77–91; Vickers, H., *Great Operatic Disasters* (London: Macmillan, 1981) p. 59; Francopan, P., *The Silk Roads* (London: Bloomsbury 2016) p. 163; Steen, M., *The Lives and Times of the Great Composers* (Cambridge: Icon Books, 2003) ch. 27.

Puccini's Other Operas (Le Villi, Edgar, La Rondine)

Sources of quotes (some altd.):
Puccini, G., *Le Villi* and *Edgar* Vocal Scores (Milan: Ricordi 1984); *La Rondine* Vocal Score (Milan: Casa Musicale Sonzogno 1945); Carner, M, Puccini (London: Duckworth, 1974) pp. 39, 41, 43, 50, 113, 205, 207, 209, 275, 306, 310, 312, 313, 415, 416, 418; *New Grove Dictionary of Music and Musicians* (ed. S. Sadie), (London: Macmillan, 1980) vol. 11, p. 486 Maestro; vol. 15, Puccini (M. Carner) pp.431, 433; vol. 15, pp 851, 853 Ricordi (R.Macnutt); vol. 18, p. 549 Tamagno (E. Forbes).
Other sources:
New Grove Dictionary of Opera (ed. S. Sadie), (London: Macmillan, 1992) vol. 2, pp. 9, 10; vol. 2, p.252; vol. 4, pp.1010, 1011 (J Budden); *New Oxford Companion to Music* (ed. D. Arnold) (Oxford: Oxford University Press, 1983) pp. 604, 764, 1093,1118, 1484, 1507, 1516; Phillips-Matz, M-J., *Verdi* (Oxford: OUP 1993) pp. 682, 690; Lang, P.H., *Music in Western Civilisation* (London:J. M. Dent and Sons Ltd, 1963) p. 878; *Encyclopaedia Britannica* ninth edition, vol. vi, p. 521 (Courtray); J. Richardson, *The Courtesans: The Demi-Monde in 19th-Century France* (London: Weidenfeld and Nicolson, 1967), p. 82; http://www.unz.org/Pub/MussetAlfred-1908v01-00205; Friedrich. O., *Olympia: Paris in the Age of Manet* (London: Aurum Press, 1992). p. 222; Melitz, L: *The Opera Goer's Complete Guide* (London: J. M. Dent 1925) p. 214; Gombrich, E: *The Story of Art* (London: Phaidon, 1963) p. 416.

Puccini – Life and Puccini's Place as a Composer – a View

Sources of quotes (some altd), and other sources:
Barrie Jones, J. (transl. and ed.), *Gabriel Fauré: a Life in Letters* (London: Batsford, 1988) pp. 103, 111; Stassinopoulos, A., *Maria* (London: Weidenfeld & Nicolson, 1980) p. 220; Lang, P. H., *Music in Western Civilisation*(London: J. M. Dent and Sons Ltd, 1963) p. 999; Carner, M, *Puccini* (London: Duckworth, 1974. 2nd edition) pp. 366, 43, 364, 245 et seq, 283 et seq, 386; Kobbé, G., *The Complete Opera Book* (London: G. P. Putnam's Sons, 1930) p. 673; Puccini, G., *La Bohème*, full score (Milan: Ricordi, 1999) pp 90, 97; *New Grove Dictionary of Music and Musicians* (ed. S. Sadie), (London: Macmillan, 1980) vol. 15, Puccini (M Carner) pp. 432, 433; P. Wapnewski and C. Dahlhaus in Müller, U. and Wapnewski, P.(trans. J. Deathridge), *The Wagner Handbook* (Cambridge, MA: Harvard University Press, 1992 p. 113; Steen, M., *The Lives and Times of the Great Composers*(Cambridge: Icon Books, 2003), and other sources elsewhere in the text.

***

INDEX: VARIOUS ARIAS ETC

GENERAL INDEX

Short Guides
to Great Operas

Various guides to individual operas are available as ebooks:

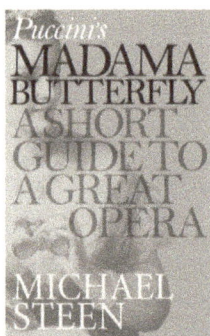

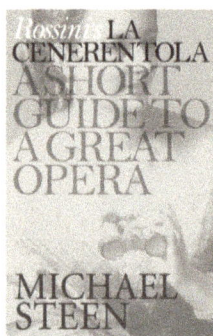

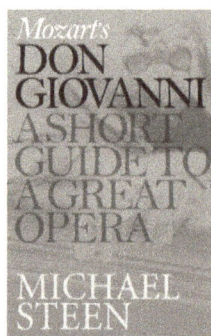

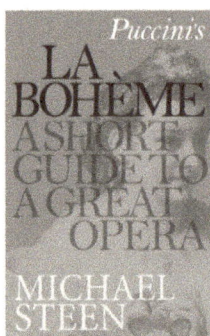

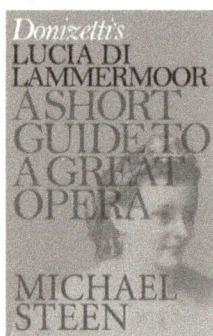

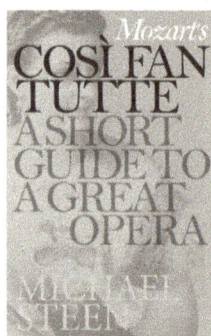

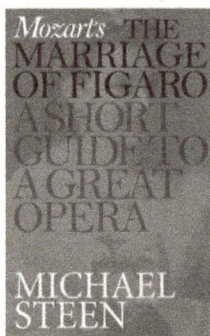

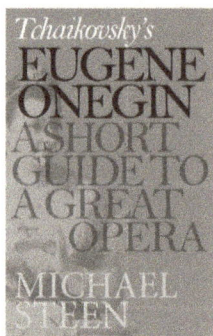

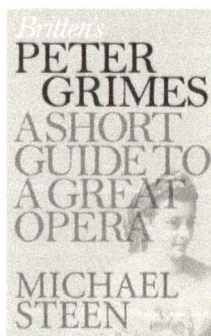

Puccini's
MADAMA BUTTERFLY
A SHORT GUIDE TO A GREAT OPERA
MICHAEL STEEN

Rossini's **LA CENERENTOLA**
A SHORT GUIDE TO A GREAT OPERA
MICHAEL STEEN

Mozart's
DON GIOVANNI
A SHORT GUIDE TO A GREAT OPERA
MICHAEL STEEN

Puccini's
LA BOHÈME
A SHORT GUIDE TO A GREAT OPERA
MICHAEL STEEN

Donizetti's
LUCIA DI LAMMERMOOR
A SHORT GUIDE TO A GREAT OPERA
MICHAEL STEEN

Mozart's
COSÌ FAN TUTTE
A SHORT GUIDE TO A GREAT OPERA
MICHAEL STEEN

Mozart's **THE MARRIAGE OF FIGARO**
A SHORT GUIDE TO A GREAT OPERA
MICHAEL STEEN

Tchaikovsky's
EUGENE ONEGIN
A SHORT GUIDE TO A GREAT OPERA
MICHAEL STEEN

Britten's
PETER GRIMES
A SHORT GUIDE TO A GREAT OPERA
MICHAEL STEEN

See greatoperas.net for more information

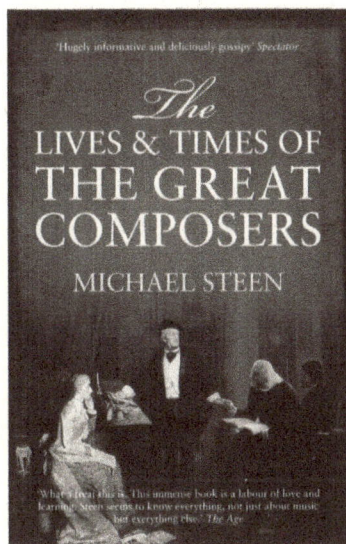

Enchantress of Nations

Pauline Viardot:
Soprano, Muse and Lover

MICHAEL STEEN

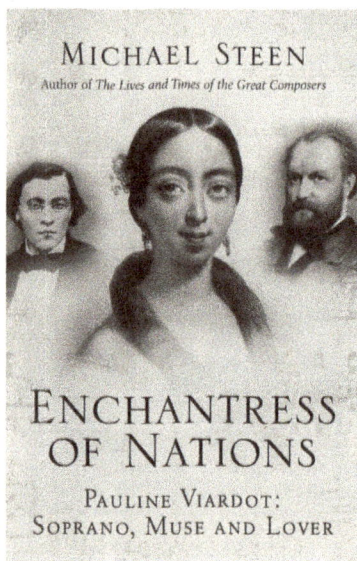

This is a picturesque but painstakingly researched biography
of the life – and the times – of the nineteenth century's
Maria Callas. She was among 'the most brilliant dramatic stars
of our time', according to Franz Liszt, and billed as 'the most
talked of opera singer in Europe'. *Enchantress of Nations* is a
lavish biography of this amazing woman whose life spanned most
of the nineteenth century; and it also weaves a rich tapestry of
music and literature in France, England and Russia.

ISBN: 9781840468434